Routledge Revivals

Economic Policy and Industrial Growth in Pakistan

Economic Policy and Industrial Growth in Pakistan (1969) is a both quantitative and analytical survey on the economic development of Pakistan. The basis of the analysis is a simple empirically verifiable model of the growth of an 'infant industry', since all of Pakistan's industries were young when the country itself was formed. The author carefully explores the intentions of government policy makers, as revealed both in their statements of policy and in their actions in setting tariffs and regulating imports. He shows how the tariff structure had little or no effect on the price structure of the country and on the pattern of industrial growth. The system of import controls is here treated to a quantitative analysis, and is related in detailed ways to the price structure and to the composition and timing of domestic output growth.

Economic Policy and Industrial Growth in Pakistan

Stephen R. Lewis Jr.

Routledge
Taylor & Francis Group

First published in 1969
by George Allen & Unwin Ltd

This edition first published in 2026 by Routledge
4 Park Square, Milton Park, Abingdon, Oxon, OX14 4RN

and by Routledge
605 Third Avenue, New York, NY 10017

Routledge is an imprint of the Taylor & Francis Group, an informa business

Publisher's Note
The publisher has gone to great lengths to ensure the quality of this reprint but points out that some imperfections in the original copies may be apparent.

Disclaimer
The publisher has made every effort to trace copyright holders and welcomes correspondence from those they have been unable to contact.

A Library of Congress record exists under LCCN: 75379223

ISBN: 978-1-041-24983-2 (hbk)
ISBN: 978-1-003-74454-2 (ebk)
ISBN: 978-1-041-24985-6 (pbk)

Book DOI 10.4324/9781003744542

Economic Policy and Industrial Growth in Pakistan

by

STEPHEN R. LEWIS, JR.

Associate Professor of Economics, Williams College, Williamstown Massachusetts

A Publication of
The Pakistan Institute of Development Economies
Karachi, Pakistan

London

GEORGE ALLEN AND UNWIN LTD

FIRST PUBLISHED IN 1969

Second impression 1970

ISBN 0 04 338034 4

PRINTED IN GREAT BRITAIN
in 10 on 12 point Times type
BY ALDEN & MOWBRAY LTD
AT THE ALDEN PRESS, OXFORD

PREFACE

This book was first conceived in the winter and spring of 1964, when I was privileged to be a Research Adviser to the Pakistan Institute of Development Economics, Karachi, and head of its Fiscal and Monetary Section. The framework for much of the book took shape, and most basic data were collected, while I was at the Institute from 1963 to 1965. My colleagues at the Institute at the time have each contributed to this effort, and the many references in the text indicate that this study could not have been complete if the staff of the Institute had not produced a set of basic studies dealing with economic policies and their consequences in Pakistan. Mushtaq Hussain, Matilal Pal, Sarfraz Qureshi, Ghulam Mohammad Radhu, all members of the Fiscal and Monetary Section of the Institute, and my fellow Advisers, Ronald Soligo and Philip Thomas, were all party to discussions of the method, the data, and the interpretation. The text references to their individual pieces of research understate the importance of their individual and collective contribution to my attempts to understand the industrialization process in Pakistan. I am most grateful to the Institute and to the Ford Foundation, which supported my stay in Pakistan through its assistance to the Institute, and which sponsored the publication of this book through a grant to the Economic Growth Center at Yale University.

During the academic year 1965/66 my continuing research on Pakistan's industrial growth was supported at the Project for Quantitative Research in Economic Development at Harvard University through a research contract with the United States Agency for International Development. From the summer of 1966, through the academic year 1966/67, and part of the summer of 1967, the drafting and revision of the manuscript were supported by a research contract between Williams College and the Agency for International Development.

To all the above institutions I am most grateful for support. The views expressed in this book are, of course, my responsibility.

Various officials and departments of the Government of Pakistan gave freely of their time and made available extensive unpublished material and worksheets, without which this and earlier studies could not have been completed. The Central Board of Revenue and the Central Statistical Office were particularly helpful. At the Planning Commission, Moinuddin Baqai was especially generous in helping me understand Pakistan and her problems. Richard Gilbert, Asbjorn Bergan, Joseph Stern, and Wouter Tims of the Harvard Advisory Group to the Planning Commission often offered their thoughts on methods and results, and always co-operated in providing relevant information. Joseph Stern aided beyond the bounds of friendship or duty in providing interpretation and communication with other associates at the Institute in the year after I left Pakistan.

Earlier drafts of this book were read by several people, and their comments and discussions were of great value in revising the manuscript. Henry Bruton, Hollis Chenery, Walter Falcon, Edward Mason, John Power, Maurice Scott, and Gordon Winston all made extremely useful comments. Ronald Soligo bears special mention because he and I have discussed the project regularly from its inception to its completion, and his comments on earlier drafts of the manuscript were always exceedingly useful. All these men have contributed notably to any precision the argument of the book may have acquired.

I have enjoyed considerable assistance in the preparation of the materials and the processing of the monograph. Doris Dodge did a monumental job of amassing and analysing data at Harvard during 1965/66, found time to question methods and approach and to comment on style and argument, and provided able assistance in virtually every area of the study. Assistance with computations was also provided by Leonard De Souza in Karachi, Hazel Elkington at Harvard, and Sara Clark at Williams. Several typists have coped with my illegible handwriting, but I would particularly like to acknowledge the assistance of Carol Wilson and Elizabeth Howarth who typed full drafts of the manuscript at the final stages.

A special debt is owed to three men. Nurul Islam, Director of the Institute, actively encouraged the completion and publication of this volume under the sponsorship of the Institute. He also commented on much of the work that went into the book. Mark Leiserson has been both sympathetic and ruthless in his substantive criticism of my work, and has been generous without limit in giving his time and his encouragement since I arrived in Karachi in 1963. I am grateful for both his friendship and his advice. Emile Despres has shaped my education in economics, as well as much of my professional experience, much more than any other person or group of persons. He has been teacher, critic, adviser, and friend for as long as I have studied economics. If I have succeeded in asking the right questions in this study, it is due largely to his patient attemps to educate me in the ways of an economist.

While I fully appreciate the assistance received from all those listed above, the responsibility for the views expressed, the inadequacies of the argument, or any mistakes in calculations or data rests with me.

My wife, Gayle, and my daughters enjoyed with me the experience of living in Pakistan. Gayle has shared with me the joys of encouraging results, and the discouraging times of those days when one does not seem to be making sense or progress. I thank her for sharing with me the high spots and the low ones. This book is dedicated to the memory of her parents, Edward and Nellie Foster, whose rich and inspiring lives were ended tragically and suddenly while this study was being drafted.

CONTENTS

TABLES

Tables

FIGURES

CHAPTER I

Pakistan's Economy Since Partition: Facts and Issues

In the fifteen year period 1949/50–1964/65, the rate of increase in real *per capita* income in Pakistan was less than 1 per cent per year. Over the same period, the output of the modern manufacturing sector increased at an average rate of 15 per cent per year. Although the industrial base in 1949/50 was extremely small, the growth rate of industry was among the most rapid of any country in the world. The principal focus of this book is an attempt to understand the reasons for the spectacular growth in modern industry that occurred in an otherwise stagnant economy. In addition to an examination of the reasons for the rapid growth of total industrial output, the book is concerned with the explanation of differential growth rates among modern manufacturing industries. There was considerable debate and discussion in the mid-1960s about whether 'too much' growth had taken place in industries producing consumer goods, and not enough in intermediate and capital goods. An attempt is made in this book to assess the relative importance of policy variables and non-policy determinants of domestic industrial growth, since participants in the debate on industrial policy in the 1960s assumed that economic policy was a principal determinant of industrial structure.

Before spelling out precisely the questions this book tries to answer, some background is given on (i) the nature of the structural changes that occurred in Pakistan over the period after Partition, (ii) the broad outlines of policy formulation in that period, and (iii) a brief statement of my interpretation of the industrialization that took place. After the general background and the nature of the enquiry have been laid out, Chapter II gives a brief formal treatment of the analytical model underlying much of the empirical analysis. Chapter III deals with the growth of the manufacturing sector as a whole, and of three major subsectors of manufacturing: industries producing primarily (*a*) consumption goods, (*b*) intermediate goods, and (*c*) investment and related goods. Chapters IV and V include a discussion of the policy variables associated with industrial growth, and an attempt to relate quantitatively growth of industrial sectors and subsectors to major policy variables. Chapter VI disaggregates the analysis of industrialization. It was possible to collect data for as many as twenty-six manufacturing industries for periods of 10–15 years. Output, imports, exports, and such policy variables as domestic tax rates, tariffs, and import licensing decisions are examined at a more detailed level of analysis. The final chapter contains a summary of the evidence on industrial growth and an evaluation of the various arguments that have either attacked or supported the directions of government policy and the structure of modern industry that developed in the 1950s and 1960s.

1. MAJOR STRUCTURAL CHANGES IN PAKISTAN, 1947–65

Pakistan was created in 1947 by the Partition of former British India. About 7 million people migrated to Pakistan from India, and vice versa, amid a religious and social war that took hundreds of thousands of lives. The best trained government administrators, academicians, businessmen, and much of the financial community were primarily non-Muslims, who migrated to or stayed in India, rather than in Muslim Pakistan. The new nation of Pakistan, now the fifth largest in the world, with a population in the mid-1960s over 110 million, is split geographically into two parts by a hostile nation four times her size. Over 1,000 miles of land, or a 3,000 mile sea voyage, separate the two wings. While measures of the level of real *per capita* income are subject to wide margins of error, estimates of sixty to eighty U.S. dollars per head indicate the right order of magnitude. Agriculture was and is the dominant source of income and is even more dominant in employment, supporting almost 75 per cent of the labour force in 1961. Agricultural output has been subject to wide fluctuations, and East Pakistan particularly has always suffered from severe floods and catastrophic cyclones. Defence expenditures have been large, due to hostile neighbours on virtually all sides, which placed a heavy burden on a poor country. Political instability plagued the new nation up to 1958, when martial law was declared and a new era of political stability was ushered in under the leadership of Field Marshal Mohammad Ayub Khan.

Growth rates for real output of various sectors and for income *per capita* are given in Table 1. In the decade before 1960, total GNP

TABLE 1. *Annual Compound Growth Rates by Sector at 1959/60 Factor Cost (per cent, per year)*

	Pre-Plan Period 1949/50–1954/55	*First Plan 1954/55–1959/60*	*Second Plan 1959/60–1964/65*
Agriculture	1·3	1·4	3·5
'M' sector	9·7	6·4	11·9
(Large-scale manufacturing)	(23·6)	(9·3)	(13·1)
'S' sector	2·5	2·7	5·5
GNP	2·6	2·4	5·3
Population	2·5	2·5	2·6
GNP *per capita*	0·2	0	2·7

Notes: 'M' Sector includes the following: mining, manufacturing, construction and production of electricity and gas.

'S' Sector is all that is not included in the other two.

Data sources: all figures taken from or computed from T. M. Khan and A. Bergan, 'Measurement of Structural Change in the Pakistan Economy: A Review of the National Income Estimates, 1949/50–1963/64', *Pakistan Development Review*, Summer 1966. 1949/50 figures were trend values for the decade 1949/50–1959/60, for Agriculture and for GNP. 'M' and 'S' are 1949/50 actuals. 1954/55 figures are a 3 year average centred on 1954/55. 1959/60 figures are trend values from 1959/60 to 1964/65 as given by Khan and Bergan, Tables IV, V and VI.

growth barely kept up with, and food production certainly lagged behind, population increases. The modern sector, composed of manufacturing, construction, mining, and production of electricity and gas, grew considerably faster than the rest of the economy. 'Large-scale' manufacturing industry[1] grew at rates that bordered on the spectacular. The slowest period of growth for manufacturing was during the First Plan period (1955–60), when it increased only

[1] By census definition a large-scale industry employs more than twenty workers and uses power.

9·3 per cent per year. In the Second Five Year Plan period, all sectors grew more rapidly than in the preceding 5 years; agricultural production began to outstrip population growth; and national income *per capita* rose over 2·5 per cent per year. The extent to which the Second Plan period constitutes a change in trend or a deviation from a continuing low trend is still not known.

The differential growth rates of the various sectors of the economy are reflected in the changing structure of the economy shown in Table 2. Agriculture declined in importance from almost

Table 2. Industrial Distribution of GNP in Pakistan, Factor Cost of 1959/60

	1949/50	*1954/55*	*1959/60*	*1963/64*
Agriculture	59·9%	56·0%	53·4%	48·9%
Manufacturing, mining, construction and public utilities	7·1	9·9	12·0	16·2
All other	33·0	34·1	34·6	34·9
Total GNP	100·0%	100·0%	100·0%	100·0%
Population (millions)	77·6	87·6	98·9	112·4
GNP *per capita* (Rs.)	315	318	317	362

Source: Khan and Bergan, *op. cit.* See Table 1 for details.

60 per cent of GNP in 1949/50 to less than half of GNP in 1964/65. The manufacturing, mining, construction and public utilities sector more than doubled its share of output from 7·1 to 16·2 per cent of GNP over the same 15 year period. The aggregate figures hide an important characteristic of the economy of Pakistan, namely the differences in industrial structure and income levels between the East and West wings. The East wing is more heavily agricultural (55·5 per cent of Gross Provincial Product in the East *vs.* 42·9 per cent in the West in 1964/65). The level of *per capita* income, according to the best available estimates,[1] was over 30 per cent higher in West than in East Pakistan in 1964/65, though it had been only 10 per cent higher in 1949/50. East Pakistanis complained that not only were they less well off at the time of Partition, but they also had been exploited by the West wing to provide resources for development in that richer province. Some evidence on this issue is given in later chapters.

[1] Khan and Bergan, *op. cit.*

The changes in economic structure are also brought out clearly in the behaviour of saving and investment as shown in Table 3. The investment rate more than doubled during the 1950s, even though there was no increase in *per capita* income. During the first half of the 1960s investment rose to over 18 per cent of GNP. The share of gross saving in GNP rose less spectacularly, though it, too, more

TABLE 3. *Shares of Principal Aggregates in GNP at Current Factor Cost*

	1949/50	*1954/55*	*1959/60*	*1964/65*
Domestic saving	4·6	6·8	8·8	12·6
Domestic investment	4·6	8·5	11·8	18·8
Commodity imports	7·2	5.4	7·7	11·7
Commodity exports	7·7	6·5	5·3	5·4

Note: Saving and investment for 1949/50 and 1954/55 are computed at constant factor cost of 1959/60. GNP at 1959/60 factor cost is used as the denominator for these figures. No other reliable data are available.

Source: Domestic saving and investment: 1949/50 and 1954/55 from Planning Commission, *The Third Five Year Plan, 1965–70*, Karachi, June 1965, p. 7. 1959/60 and 1964/65 from Planning Commission, *Final Evaluation of the Second Five Year Plan (1960–65)*, Rawalpindi, December 1966, p. 9.

Commodity imports and exports: 3 year averages centred on the year given in the Table. Imports and exports from Ministry of Finance, *Pakistan Economic Survey 1966/67*, Rawalpindi, 1967. GNP figures from CSO, *Monthly Statistical Bulletin*, June 1967.

than doubled in the 15 years from 1949/50 to 1964/65.[1] The reason that investment rose more rapidly than saving, particularly after 1955, was the increased inflow of foreign aid. This is reflected by the widening gap between commodity imports and commodity exports in the period after 1955. The declining importance of exports in GNP over the 1950s is due in part to falling prices for Pakistan's principal exports, but there was also a reduction in the quantum of some exports, particularly cotton and tea. Commodity imports were

[1] There are severe problems with the accuracy of both the saving and the investment estimates. It is fairly clear, however, that both saving and investment have been rising as a percentage of GNP, though putting a precise number on either one is not possible. See my article 'Domestic Resources and Fiscal Policy in Pakistan's Second and Third Plans', *Pakistan Development Review*, Autumn 1965.

limited by export earnings before foreign assistance began to flow substantially in the late 1950s. The gap between imports and exports (and between investment and domestic saving) widened sharply in the 1960s.

The combination of the changing industrial distribution of output and the changing composition of product use is reflected in the structure of imports and exports. Table 4 gives the relative importance of four groups of commodities that reflect the other movements quite well. The principal use of foreign exchange in the immediate

TABLE 4. *Importance of Certain Commodity Groups in Total Imports (percentages)*

	1951/52	*1959/60*	*1964/65*
Cotton yarn and cloth	28·7	0·6	*a*
Grains and flour	*a*	14·6	12·7
Iron and Steel and products thereof	7·4	8·7	16·6
Machinery, transport and electrical equipment	9·2	25·4	33·4
Value of commodity imports (Rs. million)	2,237·3	2,461·0	5,392·4

a Less than 0·5 per cent.

Source: 1951/52 and 1959/60 from CSO, *Statistical Yearbook 1963*, Karachi, 1964. 1964/65 from CSO, *Monthly Statistical Bulletin*, September 1965.

post-Partition period was for imports of manufactured consumer goods, principally cotton textiles. For 1951/52, the first year for which standardized statistics are available, these goods alone accounted for over one-quarter of imports. Imports of food grains were insignificant, reflecting Pakistan's role as a bread-basket for India before Partition. Goods connected with the modern manufacturing sector, either as inputs or as capital goods, were only a small part of total imports. By 1959/60, there was a completely different pattern. Products closely associated with capital formation and with modern manufacturing (machinery, electrical goods, and transport equipment) accounted for one-quarter of imports, while imports of cotton textiles had virtually disappeared. Grains and flour had become almost 15 per cent of total commodity imports, reflecting the excess of population growth over food production increases in the 1950s. In the 1960s the changes continued, and products of the metal-working and equipment industries totalled half of commodity imports. Grains continued to be important, though less so than in 1959/60. One should recall that these sharp changes in structure occurred in the 1950s with a fall in the quantum of imports, and in the 1960s with a doubling of total imports in less than 5 years.

The composition of exports changed considerably over the same period, as shown in Table 5. Raw jute, produced in East Pakistan,

TABLE 5. *Composition of Principal Commodity Exports from Pakistan (percentages)*

	Pre-Plan 1951/52–1954/55	*First Plan 1955/56–1959/60*	*Second Plan 1960/61–1964/65*
Raw jute	46·1	47·3	39·2
Raw cotton	38·6	18·4	14·0
Wool, hides and skins	5·5	7·8	7·4
Jute and cotton textiles	0·7	14·0	20·2
Other exports	9·2	12·5	19·2
TOTAL	100·1	100·0	100·0

Source: Computed from: *Statistical Yearbook, 1963*, pp. 163–4, for 1951/52–1959/60, *Final Evaluation Report*, p. 164, 1960/61–1964/65.

was the most important earner of foreign exchange throughout the 15 years, though it declined somewhat in relative importance in the 1960s. Raw cotton earnings were nearly as important as those from jute in the early 1950s, but fell to about one-third the importance of jute by the 1960s. The major increases in exports were from the newly established manufacturing industries. Jute and cotton textiles, which replaced competing imports by the mid-1950s, began to produce export surpluses by the late 1950s and early 1960s. Other minor manufactures followed a similar pattern, accounting for a part of the rise in 'other exports'. The latter category was also bolstered by increased exports of fish and fine quality rice.

The exceedingly rapid growth of modern manufacturing during the 1950s, amid a relatively stagnant economy, particularly in agriculture, was reflected in the decline of imports of some manufactured goods, the rise of those imports related to investment activity, the emergence of certain manufactured exports, the conversion from an export surplus to an import surplus in food grains, and the decline of agricultural exports that were used as raw materials by domestic industries. In the 1960s the changes in the structure of production were somewhat smaller, and in different directions due to the increased flows of aid-financed imports and the more rapid growth of such sectors as agriculture.

The change in economic structure over the 15 years from the early 1950s to the mid-1960s was substantial, even though there was little change in the level of *per capita* income. To the extent that structural changes are usually associated with changes in *per capita* income levels (the usual measure of 'development') the experience in Pakistan might be broadly consistent with any of three phenomena. (i) The economy was in 'equilibrium' in the early years, with a production structure appropriate to its income level and resource endowment, and it moved into a 'disequilibrium' over the 1950s and 1960s. (ii) The economy was in a 'disequilibrium' in the early 1950s, given its income, resources and economic structure, and the major changes in structure without much real income growth were due to a readjustment of the economy toward a more 'equilibrium' structure. (iii) The economy was in equilibrium in both periods, but conditions such as technology and foreign prices had changed so that a very different productive structure was consistent with a similar level of *per capita* income and resource endowment. The relationships between productive structure, resources, and income levels, however, are affected by economic policy. Thus, the extent of equilibrium or disequilibrium among the real economic variables is markedly affected by the economic policy a government adopts. It is important, therefore, to understand the principal directions of government policy in Pakistan over the years after Partition.

2. MAJOR POLICY MEASURES IN PAKISTAN, 1947–65

The details of changes in economic policy in Pakistan in the period up to 1965 are discussed in later chapters, but some salient features must be brought out in order to understand the questions this book tries to answer. The Partitition of the subcontinent broke up a customs union of Pakistan and India.[1] The hostility with which India and Pakistan viewed each other is also an important dimension of the economic policies adopted by Pakistan. It is conceivable that after Partition the two countries might have continued to trade with one another and to remain in a customs union, but this did not happen. Tariff and non-tariff barriers were quickly erected between the two countries, and trade virtually came to a standstill in 1949. The proximate cause of the cessation of trade was the decision of Pakistan not to devalue its rupee following the devaluation of the pound sterling and the Indian rupee in 1949.

The full effects of the decision not to devalue in 1949, which left the Pakistani rupee greatly overvalued,[2] were not felt immediately for two reasons. First, Pakistan could use sterling balances left from World War II to finance imports from abroad without exporting a similar value of goods. Second, the sharp rise in raw material prices during the Korean War boom meant rapid but very temporary increases in export earnings from raw jute and raw cotton. From 1950 to 1952, there were relatively free imports of most goods, subject only to tariff restrictions and the restrictions imposed by the cutback of trade with India. In 1952, following the deterioration of jute and cotton prices and falling export earnings, Pakistan faced a serious trade crisis and sharply falling reserves. Again, however, the government decided not to devalue the currency, and instead chose to keep payments in balance by the use of a set of detailed physical controls on imports and exports, accompanied by strict exchange controls. Tariffs were maintained, but they were not the major determinant of prices or of import composition. Export taxes on jute and cotton were raised during the Korean War boom, and were lowered somewhat following the fall in prices. Exporters of such commodities received low rupee prices for their goods both because the currency was overvalued and because of the export taxes.

[1] The basic source of the analysis of Partition and its economic effects is M. A. Rahman, *Partition, Integration, Economic Growth and Interregional Trade*, Karachi, 1963.

[2] Evidence on the overvaluation of Pakistan's Rupee is given in Chapters IV and V.

Tight quantitative controls on imports and controls on foreign exchange transactions were maintained throughout the 1950s. They were supplemented by controls on domestic prices of some manufactured goods and, late in the 1950s, agricultural goods as well. In 1955, the official price of the rupee was changed to par with the Indian rupee (Rs. 4.76 per U.S. dollar), but considerable excess demand for imports continued, and quantitative controls remained the binding constraint on import levels and composition. Exporters were given some additional incentives in 1959 through a multiple exchange rate system known as the Export Bonus Scheme. The effective price of foreign exchange was raised by 20–60 per cent for exporters of various products not including raw cotton and jute. 1959 also marked the beginning of a series of changes in economic policy away from direct and towards indirect controls on imports and on domestic prices of other goods. A number of measures were taken in import licensing that made market forces more important in determining the commodity composition of imports and the distribution of ownership of import licences.[1] Finally, in 1964 the government took the first step towards real elimination of direct controls by allowing the import of certain items from the United States (under an aid agreement) without the presentation of an import licence. The decreased reliance on direct controls was accompanied by a large increase in the flow of aid resources and in the ratio of imports to GNP.

The attitude of the government throughout the 1950s was generally favourable to private investment. At the same time, however, there was considerable hostility on the part of many government officials towards the results that the market gave in the determination of prices and in the allocation of resources. A combination of private ownership and public direction of the economy was the guiding principle of economic policy, though the direction was not particularly systematic.[2] There was a preference for investments that

[1] These developments are discussed by P. S. Thomas, 'Import Licensing and Import Liberalization in Pakistan', *Pakistan Development Review*, Winter 1966.

[2] A most interesting discussion of controls on the private sector is given by M. Haq in *The Strategy of Economic Planning: A Case Study of Pakistan*, Karachi, 1963, pp. 49–55.

promised to save foreign exchange almost without regard to the costs involved, a desire to produce domestically almost anything that technologically could be produced there. The government made implicit (and sometimes explicit) assumptions that both the demand for Pakistan's exports and Pakistan's demand for imports were price inelastic. Consequently, the idea of changing the price of foreign exchange in order to decrease its use or to increase its availability did not receive much support. This is particularly evident in the Report of the Economic Appraisal Committee in 1952.

The main lines of development of policy-making bodies and planning organizations indicate a marked movement both towards better and more comprehensive discussions of economic policy and towards better staffed and more highly respected bodies to make such policy.[1] The first planning attempt was the Six Year Development Program of 1951–57, which was drawn up in 3 months in 1950. It was little more than a general statement about goals and a list of specific projects. The Economic Appraisal Committee in 1952 gave an authoritative statement of government policy, which is examined in Chapter IV, but it did little in the way of planning (in any of the accepted uses of that term). The first efforts at comprehensive planning were begun in 1953, with the appointment of a Planning Board. With the aid of a staff of foreign advisers, it drew up the First Five Year Plan (1955–60), but the Plan was not even approved until after a year of the Plan period had elapsed. The First Plan document was a comprehensive and weighty volume stating the problems the country faced and some solutions to them. Its suggestions and analyses were largely ignored until after martial law was declared. Through the late 1950s, however, the staff of the Planning Commission began to take shape, and it became a centre for the activity of those promoting a movement away from direct controls of the economy and those favouring greater care in planning and a greater effort at development.

The Second Five Year Plan, which was published in June 1960, presented a series of proposals and arguments in favour of dismantling the control system and replacing it with controls operating through the tax system and the pricing of foreign exchange. With

[1] Some material in this paragraph is based on A. Waterson, *Planning in Pakistan*, Baltimore, 1963.

few exceptions, however, there was little in either of the Plans that laid out both the directions in which the economy ought to move and the means for directing resources in such a manner. In the Second Plan period there was an Industrial Investment Schedule to keep sanctioned industrial expansion in line with Plan objectives, but the Schedule was oversubscribed generally and was undersubscribed in a great many industries, so that it did not prove to be a very effective measure for directing resources.[1] During the Second Plan period, the annual budget of the government referred more and more to the proposals in the Plan document, and the Plan did have more effect on government resource allocation than it had in earlier years. A major feature of the Second Plan period, however, was the rise of the Planning Commission and its staff to a place high in the economic councils of the government, and the increase in the amount of influence the Planning Commission had in determining economic policies. One should remember, however, that much of the structural change that occurred in Pakistan took place before there was an effective planning organization that had any influence on policy, and that the 1950s were a period in which direct controls were dominant in allocating resources. Detailed industrial planning and attempts to relate policy changes to intended industrial growth patterns are features of the Third Plan (1965–70) that were absent from the earlier efforts.

3. A VIEW OF INDUSTRIAL GROWTH AND QUESTIONS TO BE EXPLORED

The two major factors determining the course of industrial growth in Pakistan in the 1950s and into the early 1960s were: (i) the Partition of the subcontinent, and (ii) the decision by the government of Pakistan not to devalue in 1949 or 1952 but to rely on exchange controls and quantitative restrictions to control imports. Partition

[1] For this reason, the investment schedule and licensing procedures are ignored in the rest of this monograph. A preliminary evaluation of the functioning of the sanction procedures during the Second Plan is given by M. T. Durrani, *The Pattern of Private Industrial Investment During the Second Five Year Plan*, Research Report No. 54, Pakistan Institute of Development Economics, Karachi, 1966.

left Pakistan a surplus area in food and agricultural raw materials and a deficit area in manufactures of all types. Even if economic policy had been scrupulously neutral (if the government had, for example, adopted a floating exchange rate with no tariff barriers) it is likely that industrial growth would have been relatively fast simply because of Partitition which destroyed the customs union. Changes in the industrial structure of the economy would have occurred more rapidly than would be expected from the growth of *per capita* income alone. Government policy was not neutral, however, but decidedly favoured industrialization, particularly through the decision not to devalue. Given the productive structure that existed at Partition, the trade policy adopted turned the terms of trade sharply against agriculture. When agricultural goods which were normally exported were given unfavourable exchange rates, and when imports of manufactured goods were markedly curtailed, the disequilibrium that existed in the markets for these goods was removed by drastic changes in relative prices. Manufactured goods' prices rose, while agricultural goods' prices fell. The change in relative prices, however, created a disequilibrium between the prices of manufactured goods in domestic markets and the costs of producing such goods (particularly when they used agricultural raw materials). This latter disequilibrium contained the mechanism for its own removal: high profitability of producing those goods in short supply. In terms of simple market theory, the rate of profit in manufacturing industries greatly exceeded the 'normal' rate. The high profits induced individuals to enter manufacturing activities and expand the supply of manufactured goods. The expansion of productive capacity in manufactured goods eventually drove prices of the goods down towards long-run average costs in manufacturing industries. The very rapid rate of industrial growth in the 1950s, therefore, can be best understood in terms of an economy working off the disequilibrium created both by the Partition of the subcontinent and by the trade policies adopted by the government of Pakistan in the early to mid-1950s.

Turning the terms of trade against agriculture had two kinds of effects on the industrial sector. First, incentives to invest in manufacturing activities rose sharply. Second, the more favourable terms of trade for manufacturing implicitly taxed the agricultural sector and transferred income to the industrial sector, particularly to industrial profits. There is little systematic evidence available on saving by sector or of rates of reinvestment, but such evidence as does exist[1] suggests that the gross reinvestment rates out of manufacturing profits were in the vicinity of 75 per cent. If this is true, the reason for the reasonably high marginal rate of saving (around 17 per cent over the entire period 1949/50–1964/65) in the absence of increased *per capita* incomes in the country must have been largely in the redistribution of income into the sector with the high marginal propensity to save. This is precisely the result one would expect to find if the economy fitted the widely used two-sector model of a developing economy elaborated by W. Arthur Lewis.[2]

Since income levels did not rise much, and manufacturing output grew at rates several times that of agriculture, one would expect the relative prices of the faster growing sector to fall.[3] In Pakistan, there was a fall in the prices of manufactured goods relative to the prices of agricultural goods in the period of rapid industrial growth after the trade crisis. In addition to the movements in the terms of trade between sectors, however, there is also an important question of how favourable manufacturers' terms of trade were relative to a situation of free international trade and no protection. While it is true that the terms of trade of manufacturing deteriorated over the 10 years 1954–64, manufacturing continued to be highly protected even at the end of the period. Various aspects of industrial growth and the changes in relative prices that accompanied it are analysed in Chapters III–VI. The view of the industrialization process as working off a substantial disequilibrium is the central focus of the book.

There are three separate sub-questions to be answered in finding the reason for the extremely rapid rate of industrial growth. (i) What were the effects of Partition? (ii) What were the effects of the non-

[1] G. F. Papanek, 'Industrial Production and Investment in Pakistan', *Pakistan Development Review*, Autumn 1964; K. Haq and M. Baqai, 'Savings and Financial Flows in the Corporate Sector, 1959–1963', *Pakistan Development Review*, Autumn 1967.

[2] W. A. Lewis, 'Economic Development with Unlimited Supply of Labour', The Manchester School, May 1954.

[3] This is also an important theoretical property of the two-sector model, *ibid.*

policy variables in the years after Partition? (iii) What were the effects of the trade policy that was adopted in the 1950s? It is impossible to answer these questions in a rigorous empirical fashion, but the analysis will try to keep these different aspects of the explanation for the high rate of growth as separate as possible. The first sub-question is concerned with the lack of industrial capacity of any significance in 1947. Presumably, given the normal difficulties in arranging international as opposed to internal trade, profitability of domestic manufacturing would rise after the customs union was destroyed. As a result, there would have been an adjustment in productive structure within the country as more manufactures were produced domestically rather than imported. Second, given that Pakistan had been exporting some raw materials that were processed in India and re-exported to Pakistan as manufactures, one would expect an increase in domestic production greater than that 'normally' associated with income and population changes. This situation would be particularly true in such goods as cotton textiles. Third, one is interested in the additional impact of trade policy beyond the extra incentives given to investment in manufacturing by Partition and real cost advantages of some industries. What were the differential effects of the *general* scarcity of foreign exchange at the time of the trade crisis in 1952? The decision not to devalue, but to rely on import controls to keep payments in balance, necessarily resulted in exceedingly high profitability in manufactures and in deteriorated terms of trade for agriculture, simply due to the structure of production and imports in 1947. The combination of these three factors: (i) Partition, (ii) domestic markets for manufactures and availability of agricultural raw materials, and (iii) the nature of the policy response to the trade and payments crisis, led to the rapid rate of industrial growth. The analysis in Chapters III–VI is concerned with trying to assign relative levels of importance to these three forces.

The next problem this monograph is concerned with is: why did the structure of manufacturing industry emerge as it did? It is clear that much of the import substitution that occurred in Pakistan took place in industries producing consumption goods. This could have been due to differences among industries in any number of real cost variables: the nature of the capital requirements, the technological sophistication, the demands for skilled labour, the requirements of foreign components, the size of markets relative to efficient plant size in the industry. Differential import replacement might also be due to any number of policy related variables: tariff protection, relative costs of imported components, quantitative restrictions on competing imports, advantages in direct or indirect tax treatment, or policies affecting the cost of domestically produced raw materials. The task of sorting out the relative importance of policy and non-policy variables in determining the differential growth and import substitution among Pakistan's manufacturing industries is attempted in Chapter VI.

Finally, there is a set of issues related to measuring the relative effects of policy and other factors as influences on industrial structure. One must be able to quantify the policy variables and to translate the effects of different policies into comparable measures. A number of studies undertaken in Pakistan have made contributions to this problem, and in Chapters IV–VI, I have tried to bring together the results of these and other studies and extend them somewhat in order to assess the relative importance of the policy variables that operated in Pakistan in the years since Partition.

CHAPTER II

Analysing Changes in Industrial Structure

This chapter discusses a framework for analysing industrial growth. The concern is not with the attribution of growth to various factors of production, but rather with the allocation of investment among industries. Since in Pakistan, and many other countries, disaggregated data on investment by industry are not available, the empirical portions of this book deal exclusively with industrial output. On the assumption that capacity utilization and capital output ratios are not subject to trends, the trends in output would be directly related to the allocation of investment. The principal questions of concern in the chapter and in the rest of the book are (i) why did some industries develop earlier and grow more rapidly than others, (ii) how much of the growth in various industries can be related to increased domestic demand, to import replacement, or to export demand, and (iii) how much of the direction in which resources moved can be attributed either to government policy or to more fundamental cost considerations or resource endowments? There is a heavy emphasis in the latter part of this chapter and in the empirical analysis of the rest of the book on cost and price considerations, which have generally received ample treatment in studies of static welfare but have largely been ignored in the analysis of economic growth. Since many government policy measures appear as effects on prices and costs, the introduction of such variables allows the analysis to include policy instruments in the discussion of investment allocation in response to profitability.

1. THE 'SOURCES' OF GROWTH IN MANUFACTURING OUTPUT

I am interested in part in answering the question: Can one attribute growth of industries and groups of industries to various 'causes', related either to policy or to some structural characteristic of the economy? Growth is first of all classified by 'sources' related to growth of demand and to 'import substitution'. 'Source' is intentionally kept in quotation marks, since the definition of those sources is not of universal acceptability. The method used to determine 'sources' of industrial growth is a modified version of Chenery's in 'Patterns of Industrial Growth'.[1] Import substitution is defined with reference to the proportion of imports in the total supply of an industrial good. If domestic production rises faster than imports, import substitution occurs, while if imports rise more rapidly than domestic output, the opposite of import substitution (negative import substitution?) takes place. Growth in domestic output is due to (i) the growth of demand (assuming a constant proportion of total supply is imported) and (ii) the change in the ratio of imports to total supply, or import substitution.

Other definitions might have been used, especially for import substitution. The distinctions drawn by Winston,[2] between (i) 'import substitution' that is a concomitant of growth (à la Chenery) as, for example, as market size changes, and (ii) 'import substitution' due to some set of policies to encourage temporarily uneconomic domestic production, is exceedingly important. The problem of why Pakistan had the 'import substitution' she did in various industries is discussed further in Chapters III–VI. The Chenery (proportionality) definition was adopted because of its simplicity, not for its conceptual purity. The principal competing definition of import substitution was used in analysing Pakistan's growth by A. R. Khan.[3] Khan first sets up a measure of 'normal' increase in absorption of each commodity as *per capita* income and population change. He then says that production that meets normal absorption is import substitution. Production in excess of normal absorption (if consumed domestically and not exported) is consumption liberalization. The principal difference in the two measures (whenever the share of domestic production in

[1] H. B. Chenery, 'Patterns of Industrial Growth', *American Economic Review*, September 1960.

[2] G. C. Winston, 'Notes on the Concept of Import Substitution', *Pakistan Development Review*, Spring 1967.

[3] A. R. Khan, 'Import Substitution, Export Expansion and Consumption Liberalization', *Pakistan Development Review*, Summer 1963.

total supply is rising) is that the Khan measure would call 'consumption liberalization' part of what the Chenery measure labels 'domestic demand', and the Khan measure would generally not attribute as much growth to 'import substitution' as would the proportionality measure.

The Khan measure differs (in Winston's language) essentially by adopting a different definition of 'what would have been' in the absence of 'import substitution'. The Chenery definition suggests that without import substitution both domestic production and imports would rise in the same proportion to fill any increase in total demand. The Khan definition assumes that without import substitution, any increase in demand would be met from increased imports. The Khan study of the First Plan experience suggests an indictment of the policies followed and the direction growth took. For the Second Plan period, when the growth rate accelerated and saving rose, the Khan measure would find about half of the growth of cotton textile output 'due to import substitution', even though about 99 per cent of cotton cloth supplies were produced domestically at the beginning of the Second Plan.[1] It would appear that the proportionality measure more liberally attributes growth to import substitution when import substitution, by that definition, is occurring. After the import substitution process (by the proportionality definition) is completed, it continues to go on in the Khan definition.

Since by either Khan's or Chenery's definition all increases in output must be exhausted by either domestic demand, export demand, or import substitution, the differences in the way each measure attributes growth to import substitution affects its attribution to export growth or domestic demand expansion. If an industry contains highly differentiated products, then it is quite possible that part of its output could successfully compete with exports, while imports dominate the domestic market for other goods in the industry. I have tried to separate out industries in sufficient detail

[1] Charles Vines of Harvard College, in a study of the cotton textile industry in Pakistan, recomputed Khan's results but extended them to the Second Plan period. While there is 'consumption liberalization' in the Second Plan period, the nature of Khan's definition of import substitution suggests attributing around 50 per cent of growth in cotton cloth production to 'import substitution'.

so that such occurrences are rare, but separation was not always possible. Under the Khan measure, in a mixed industry, any absolute increase in exports is attributed to export growth. Under the Chenery measure, all of an increase in exports is attributed to export growth *only* if there were no competing imports with the industry's output in the base period. Once import substitution in the Chenery (proportion of total supply) sense is complete, growth of export demand is fully credited as a 'source' of growth in the industry. If exports are expanding in an industry that is also experiencing import substitution (in the Chenery sense) a part of export growth will be credited to import substitution. For this reason, in some of the empirical sections in later chapters, the export and import substitution 'sources' are discussed together under the heading of 'trade-related growth' as differentiated from growth due only to expansion of domestic demand. I have used the proportionality definition of import substitution and concomitant definitions of domestic and export demand expansion, as shown in the next section. Questions of interpretation of the 'sources' of growth are discussed later.

Accounting for the Growth in Output[1]

First look at the growth in gross value of output due to various sources. The algebra of the method begins with

$$\Delta Z = \Delta Q \tag{2.1}$$

where Z equals total supply and Q equals total demand. Total supply is equal to domestic production X *plus* imports M, while total demand is equal to the sum of final domestic demand (including inventory accumulation) D, export demand E, and intermediate demand W. Substituting these variables into (2.1) we get:

$$\Delta X + \Delta M = \Delta D + \Delta W + \Delta E \tag{2.2}$$

or

$$\Delta X = \Delta D + \Delta W + \Delta E - \Delta M \tag{2.3}$$

Given the change in total demand, the change in domestic output

[1] This section laying out the algebra of attributing growth to various sources is drawn largely from my article with R. Soligo, 'Growth and Structural Change in Pakistan's Manufacturing Industry, 1954–1964', *Pakistan Development Review*, Spring, 1965.

which would have taken place, if there had been no import substitution is given by:

$$u_1\ (\Delta D + \Delta W + \Delta E) \qquad (2.4)$$

when $u_1 = X_1/Z_1$, i.e. the ratio of total domestic production to supply in the base period. In other words, if Pakistan continued to import in the second period the same proportion of its total supply as in the base period, the change in domestic output which would have been required to satisfy the given change in total demand is given by expression (2.4).

Expression (2.4) could be separated into three parts so that one could further ascribe changes in domestic output to changes in the various components of demand. Because there is inadequate data to allow separation of domestic final demand and intermediate demand, we have combined these into a single variable. Expression (2.4) becomes:

$$u_1\ \Delta(D+W)+u_1\ \Delta E \qquad (2.5)$$

The change in domestic output ascribed to 'import substitution' is the change in domestic output implied by the change in the proportion of total supply imported, when total demand is held constant. The total increase in output is given by:

$$\Delta X = u_1\ \Delta(D+W)+u_1\ \Delta E+(u_2-u_1)\ Z_2 \qquad (2.6)$$

where $u_2 = X_2/Z_2$, the ratio of domestic output to total supply in the later period.

The change in domestic output has now been broken into three parts: expansion of (i) domestic and (ii) export demand, when the ratio of imports to total supply is held constant at its base period level, and (iii) import substitution.

Equation (2.6) is used to isolate the components of domestic growth in some twenty-six manufacturing industries separately. The importance of these three components for the large-scale manufacturing sector as a whole is derived by summing the components for each industry:

$$\Delta X_m = \sum_i \Delta X_i = \sum_i u_{1i}\ \Delta(D_i+W_i)+\sum_i u_{1i}\ \Delta E_i+\sum_i\ (u_{2i}-u_{1i})Z_{2i} \qquad (2.7)$$

where ΔX_m is equal to the change in output of the manufacturing industries.

Equation (2.7) is also applied to various components of the manufacturing sector. All industries have been classified into one of the following three groups: (i) consumer goods, (ii) intermediate goods, and (iii) investment goods and related products. For each group we have estimated the proportion of growth in domestic output which is attributable to the three variables of equation (2.7).

The preceding discussion was carried out in terms of gross value of domestic output. Value added, however, measures the contribution of domestic factors of production to output. The changes in value added can be attributed to the same 'sources' as the changes in gross output. In addition to changes in demand it is also necessary to take account of the changing relationship between value added and gross output over time and between industries. Different ratios for different industries mean that, over time, as different industries grow at different rates, the ratio for the sector as a whole will change even if for each industry the ratio does not change.

The equation used to allocate the change in value added to various factors is given by:

$$\Delta V = u_1 r_1 \, \Delta(D+W) + u_1 r_1 \, \Delta E + (u_2 - u_1)\, r_1 Z_2 + (r_2 - r_1) u_2 Z_2 \tag{2.8}$$

where r is the ratio of value added to gross value of output at market price and V is value added.

The first two terms measure the change in value added due to the change in domestic and export demand, respectively, when both the ratio of domestic production to total supply and the proportion of value added in domestic production are the same as in the base period. The third term measures the importance of import substitution (the amount by which value added changes when the ratio of domestic production to total supply changes and when the proportion of value added to gross output remains at its base period level). The last term in equation (2.8) measures the effect on value added of changes in the ratio of value added to domestic output. The term is essentially a residual, as it measures, among other things, the effect of intra-industry changes in the composition of domestic output as well as changes in technical efficiency.

2. A SIMPLE MODEL OF 'SUCCESSFUL' IMPORT SUBSTITUTING GROWTH

The classification of growth by sources as described in the previous section has no welfare or cost dimension. In this section a simple form of welfare emphasis is introduced, with emphasis on the easy measurability of the welfare dimension that is added.

The model given below is designed to apply to any industry or subsector, and should not be thought of as applicable to, e.g., only consumer goods or intermediate products. For the sake of simplicity, the discussion of welfare neglects the very important problems of effective or implicit protection to value added, as raised by Johnson and by Balassa[1] and concentrates on nominal protection or nominal cost differentials. A discussion of effective protection is given separately in the next section. Since the model is concerned with *changing* costs, prices, and production, however, it is likely that the direction of movement in implicit and nominal protection is similar, and that the results of the model are useful for broader welfare comparisons. The variables are measured in later chapters for industries and groups of industries in Pakistan. Broadly speaking the model adds cost variables to the analysis so that 'success' is not defined as simply replacing imports by domestic production regardless of cost. The model gives an inexpensive method (in terms of data and time) of implying a picture of the efficiency with which the industrialization process has proceeded. In view of the fact that cost data are not generally available, prices have been used instead. Some problems of interpretation that arise when prices rather than costs are used are discussed below.

PHASE I: *Unrestricted Trade and an Infant Industry*

Imports (M) of the goods in question are free of duty and import licence, and are imported in sufficient quantity to allow the implicit

[1] H. G. Johnson, 'Tariffs and Economic Development', *Journal of Development Studies*, October 1964. B. Balassa, 'Tariff Protection in Industrial Countries: An Evaluation', *Journal of Political Economy*, December 1965.

exchange rate,[1] or the domestic currency price relative to the foreign price, c.i.f., to equal the official exchange rate. There is some domestic production (X_i) of the good, but it amounts to only a small fraction of the total supply (Z_i). The situation is pictured in Figure 1,

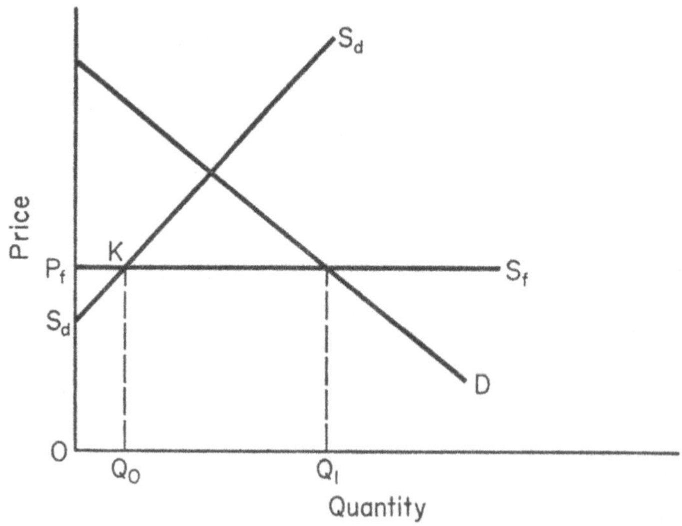

FIGURE 1. Phase I: Unrestricted trade

where S_dS_d is the short-run domestic supply curve, and P_fS_f is the foreign supply curve, so the total supply curve of the good is S_dKS_f. Total supply is OQ_1, and Q_0Q_1 is imported.

[1] Implicit exchange rates differ from purchasing power exchange rates between countries. The ratios that are computed here do not measure the purchasing power of one country's currency in terms of another, as do the Gilbert and Kravis comparisons for the United States and Western European countries, *An International Comparison of National Products and the Purchasing Power of Currencies*, Paris 1954. The ratios here are used to express the domestic market price relative to an international market price in some international medium of exchange. In the absence of controls and market distortions, the ratios of wholesale prices to f.o.b. or to c.i.f. prices should be approximately equal to the equilibrium exchange rate between the domestic currency and the medium of exchange internationally (here chosen to be the United States dollar).

PHASE IIA: *Restricted Trade: Limited High Cost Domestic Production*

Suppose a tariff is imposed on the good. The domestic price for the good would rise by the amount of the tariff, resulting in smaller imports, smaller total quantity demanded, and larger domestic supply. Since both the foreign and domestic goods are valued at the same price, there would be a rise in the share of domestic production

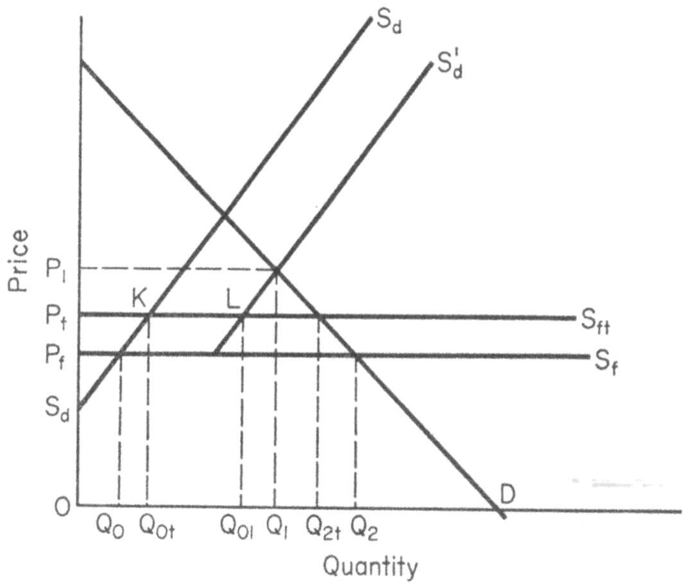

FIGURE 2. Phase IIA: Restricted trade, limited domestic production

in total supply ($X_i Z_i$), and even after this short interval, 'import substitution' in the Chenery, or proportionality, sense would have taken place.[1] The effects are shown in Figure 2. S_{ft} is the supply curve of imports after the tariff. OQ_{Ot} is produced domestically, $Q_{Ot}Q_{2t}$ is imported, and X_i/Z_i is higher than before the tariff.

[1] Note that X_i/Z_i increases, and 'import substitution' occurs for two reasons: (i) X_i increases and (ii) the total quantity demanded decreases (though Z_i may increase, decrease or remain unchanged depending on the price elasticity of demand for the good). This point is a good illustration of one of the limitations of the proportionality measure of import substitution.

Since P_t is above P_f, the implicit exchange rate for the commodity rises with protection.

For purposes of generality of exposition, suppose that a quota is also placed on imports of the good in question, as it would be in many countries, and imports are restricted to a level below what they would be with a tariff alone. If quantitative restrictions only allow $Q_{Ot}Q_{O1}$ imports into the country, the effective supply curve becomes $S_dKLS'_d$. Imports are only $Q_{Ot}Q_{O1}$ of the total supply OQ_1, so X_i/Z_i rises even farther, and the domestic price rises to P_1. The further rise in the domestic price, holding the foreign price constant, means that the introduction of quota protection for the industry results in a rise in the implicit exchange rate for this commodity above the rate implied by the tariff alone, which was, in turn, above the official rate. If other commodities were not protected (and the exchange rate remained fixed), it would mean a rise in the relative prices of the protected goods.

PHASE IIB: *Output Growth at High Cost*

What is postulated eventually is a learning curve of some sort, or economies of scale in the industry, such that as output of the protected industry is increased, the supply curve of the domestic industry will both fall and flatten out. A true infant industry should develop in such a manner. In almost any case, however, investment in the industry becomes profitable after the tariff and quantitative restrictions are imposed. The supply curve for most industries would at least shift to the right somewhat. In this phase, the supply position changes relative to domestic demand, so that *first*, virtually all of total supply is produced domestically, very little is imported, and X_iZ_i approaches say, 90 per cent or more. At this point one arrives at the important question: at what price are domestic goods being produced? Figure 3 shows a case where domestic production has completely replaced imports, but total domestic costs have remained above imported costs by the full amount of the tariff. If effective protection to value added in the industry were taken into account, the domestic resource cost would undoubtedly be much higher. The implicit exchange rate for the good is still equal to the official exchange rate plus the tariff.

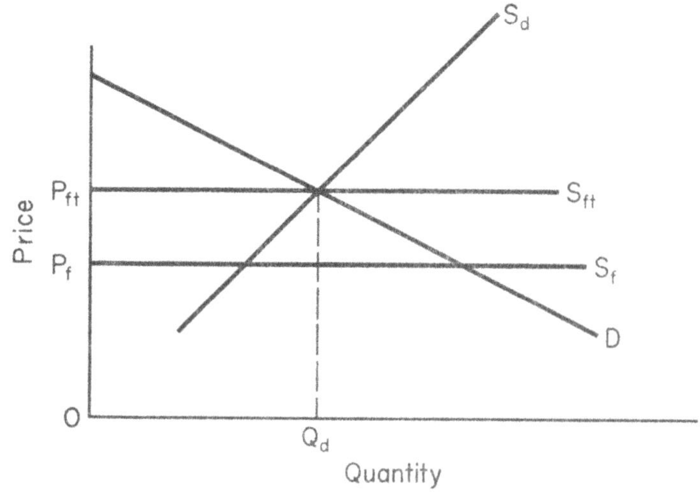

FIGURE 3. Phase IIB: Output at high cost

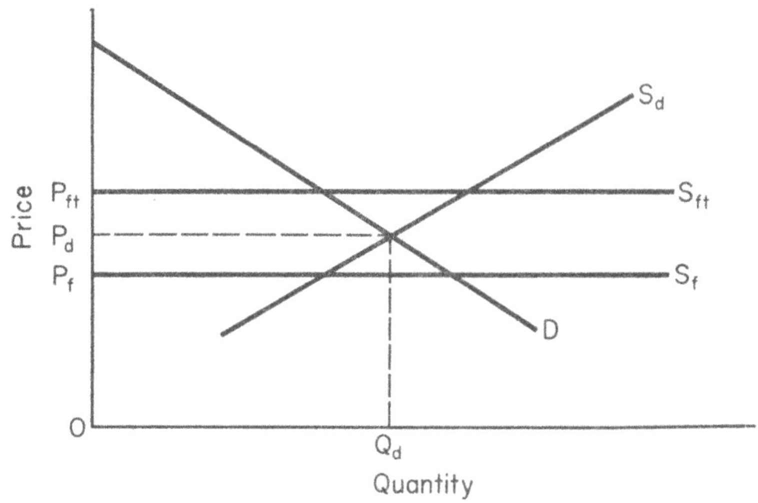

FIGURE 4. Phase III: Falling domestic costs

PHASE III: *Falling Domestic Costs*

If the industry remains in the position represented by Figure 3, or Phase IIB, there is serious question as to whether protection was justified. (A good trick, of course, is to determine beforehand whether there is any possibility of a particular industry getting past IIB!) What one would like to observe is that domestic costs fall and reduce the excess cost of producing at home what could be imported. What we would expect to observe in a 'successful' case would be that domestic prices (and domestic costs) in the industry fall, and the implicit exchange rate between the domestic price and the foreign price, c.i.f., falls below the official exchange rate adjusted for the tariff. In other words, in Phase IIB the industry supplies virtually all domestic demand. In Phase III, it lowers its costs so that the nominal tariff becomes redundant. This is shown in Figure 4, for a case where X_i/Z_i is unity, and P_d is less than P_{ft}. (In practice, X_i/Z_i is not likely to be unity, since product differences even within a narrowly defined industry are likely to result in some imports.) As tariffs begin to become redundant, one might say that the import substitution has started to become successful in a welfare sense. Imports have been reduced as a percentage of total supply, which is often thought of as the only measure of success. In addition, the welfare costs of import substitution have started to come down as cost of domestic production of importables approaches the cost of acquiring the same goods through exporting.[1]

PHASE IV: *Fully Competitive Domestic Production*

The last phase is probably the most difficult, both to achieve and to measure. Provided the industries that were protected were one in which the country had long-run comparative advantage, one would expect that one of two things would happen. The industry would develop a cost structure that would permit it either (i) to produce for domestic supply alone without any protection (i.e. tariffs, even if left on the books, would become completely redundant), or (ii) to produce in some significant measure for export demand (E_i). In either case, the implicit exchange rate for the industry would be approximately the same as the official exchange rate,[2] and X_i/Z_i

[1] Note that this refers only to nominal tariffs, not effective tariffs.

[2] There is an asymmetry here. Due to transport costs the industry

would be unity. In the latter case, E_i/Z_i would rise from zero (or near zero) to some larger fraction. If the industry were one in which the country had a very substantial comparative advantage, exports, E_i/Z_i, might even become larger than domestic absorption D_i/Z_i. The case in which the industry becomes an exporter is shown in

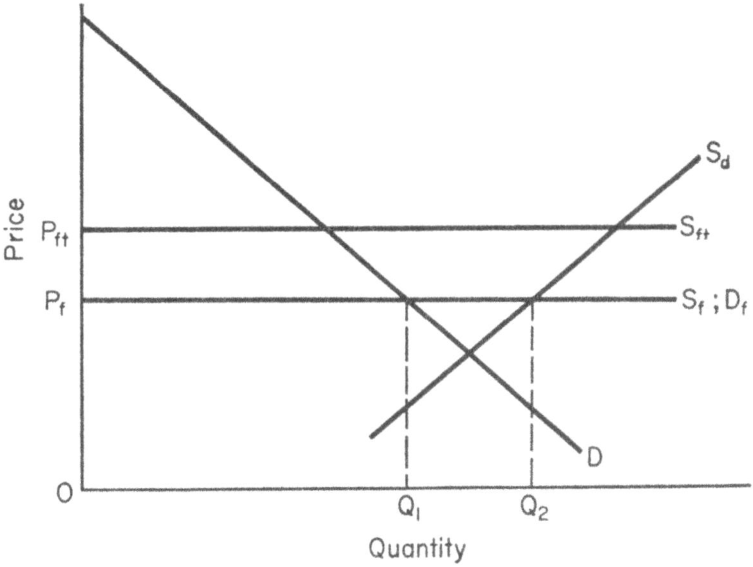

FIGURE 5. Phase IV: Fully competitive domestic production

Figure 5, where OQ_2 is domestic production, OQ_1 is domestic demand, and Q_1Q_2 is exported. The implicit exchange rate is the official rate, and the tariff is completely redundant.[1]

[1] Note that by the time Phase IV is reached, the difference between the nominal and the implicit rates of protection becomes almost meaningless, since nominal tariffs are completely redundant. If there are tariffs on inputs into the industry, however, its effective or implicit rate of protection would be negative, Indeed, the failure of an industry to have its own implicit exchange rate fall to equality with the official rate, or its failure to export successfully, may be due in some cases to the higher prices it must pay for its inputs purchased from domestic industries.

could become fully competitive with imports in the absence of tariffs but might not be able to export. The implicit exchange rate between domestic and c.i.f. prices would equal the official exchange rate but the implicit exchange rate between domestic and potential f.o.b. export price would be above the official rate.

The model describes a process of an infant industry growing up, and it does so with variables that are more or less capable of measurement. The latter fact means that the model can be used to examine industrial growth in a country and to raise some questions about the nature of the growth and, perhaps, about its efficiency. The measurable variables (given in order of ease of obtaining them) are (i) nominal tariffs, (ii) imports and exports of the industries under study, (iii) domestic production of the same industries, (iv) domestic prices in local currency, (v) c.i.f. prices of imports. The accounting 'model' for import substitution and export expansion follows that of the last sections. Changes in domestic output over time are explained as in equation (2.7) by changes in domestic demand and in exports at the base period X_i/Z_i ratio, and by import substitution, defined as changes in the X_i/Z_i ratio over the period, or:

$$\Delta X_i = \frac{X_{1i}}{Z_{1i}}(\Delta D_i) + \frac{X_{1i}}{Z_{1i}}\Delta E_i + \left\{\frac{X_{2i}}{Z_{2i}} - \frac{X_{1i}}{Z_{1i}}\right\}Z_{2i} \qquad (2.9)$$

Import substitution, the last term, is important in moving from Phase I to Phase IIB, while export expansion is important in moving from Phase III to Phase IV.

Relative prices, or more properly, relative implicit exchange rates for protected industries (P_i) and non-protected industries (P_k) would also move in predictable patterns. From Phase I to Phase IIA, P_i/P_k rises by the amount of the tariff on industry $i(t_i)$, plus any additional movement due to quantitative controls. From Phase IIB to Phase III, P_i/P_k falls to something less than $(1+t_i)$, while in moving into the 'truly successful' phase, Phase IV, P_i moves equal to P_k.

The simplest example of these movements might be the manufacturing sector relative to mining and agricultural sectors, where the former are the ith industries in which X_i/Z_i was very low traditionally, and the latter are the kth industries, where E_k/Z_k was significant, and the implicit exchange rate was very close to the official rate.

The implicit exchange rates are one way of getting at the differences between world and domestic terms of trade of the agricultural sector. If P_i is the implicit exchange rate for a manufactured good, and P_k is the rate for an agricultural good, one can obtain an average implicit rate for each sector by using some appropriate set of weights, such as the marketings of agricultural products, S_k, and the purchases of manufactured goods by the agricultural sector, B_i. Taking the ratio of the average implicit rate for agriculture $\Sigma_k P_k S_k$ to that for manufacturing $\Sigma_i P_i B_i$ would give the expression:

$$\frac{\Sigma_k P_k S_k}{\Sigma_i P_i B_i} \tag{2.10}$$

Since P_k and P_i are ratios of domestic to foreign prices, the ratio of the weighted implicit rates for the two sectors is simply the ratio of the terms of trade of the agricultural sector domestically to the terms of trade the agricultural sector *could* have had if it had been able to trade in international markets.[1] Movements in implicit exchange rates for the two sectors can tell something about movements in domestic, relative to world, terms of trade for those two sectors.

The failure of P_i/P_k to come down towards unity over some 'reasonable' period would, I think, raise questions about (i) whether the *i*th industry should have been protected, (ii) whether there are domestic market structure problems. At any point in time (since time series on P_i and P_k are not easy to come by) an array of observations for all commodities' implicit exchange rates would give authorities some idea of where to begin examining particular cases.[2] Another partial approach would be to look only at the movements of domestic relative prices over time. This movement could, or course, be misleading when foreign prices moved to offset the domestic movements, but as a first approximation it might yield results of some interest.

The model obviously assumes that domestic industry is competi-

[1] Note that the statement assumes that world offer curves are of infinite elasticity with respect to price.

[2] Obviously there are other reasons for P_i and P_k to vary among industries, as is well stated in somewhat different language by J. H. Power, 'Import Substitution as an Industrialization Strategy', *Philippine Economic Journal*, Spring 1967. At least the array of implicit exchange rates would provide a starting point for analysis, however. The model as a whole can easily be modified to take other things, such as domestic indirect tax policy, into account. E.g., P_i facing consumers might be kept high by taxes while P_i facing producers fell toward P_k, thus discouraging domestic absorption of the good as domestic costs fell, and promoting exports.

tive, not monopolistic or oligopolistic, in market structure, and that foreign supply and demand are perfectly elastic. These assumptions violate some of the principal assertions some low income countries are fond of making to explain their troubles. In choosing industries to protect, the country should be aware of the problem of establishing potential monopolists and avoid those industries in which there is an obvious danger. Also, it can be argued that tariffs that are set high initially should be lowered after some reasonable period to provide oligopolistic industries with international competition. On the problem of foreign demand, casual empiricism suggests that there is reason to doubt the allegations of 'impossibility' of breaking into foreign markets, simply on the basis that some developing countries have succeeded in doing so. At the very least, I would think, the lack of movement of manufacturing industries in a country from Phase IIB to Phases III and IV would raise some serious questions about the domestic supply conditions, or exchange rate policy, and would suggest that failure to export might not be blamed on international demand alone. Finally, there is the question of a 'reasonable' length of time in which one would expect prices and costs of import substituting industries to fall. The answer depends in part on the discount rate one chooses, and a more complete procedure for discussing it is given by Henry Bruton in his paper 'Import Substitution and Productivity Growth'.[1]

It should be noted that there are two parts to the movements of domestic costs towards the point at which they are competitive with imports, or are low enough to export. In the first place, the industry must become more efficient in using intermediate inputs and primary factors. But, in the second place, the official price of foreign exchange must be kept somewhere in line with its opportunity cost to the economy. If the exchange rate used for exports greatly overvalues the domestic currency, one should not expect domestic costs to fall low enough through increased efficiency to allow the industry to export profitably. The test of whether the industry can export profitably may be a good first approximation in answering the question: should it have been protected in the first place? It may be too harsh a test, however, if a country is maintaining a substantially

[1] H. J. Bruton, 'Import Substitution and Productivity Growth', *Journal of Development Studies*, January 1968.

overvalued currency. The inefficiency may not lie in the particular industries but in the policies being followed.

The model does not deal with a number of issues that have developed in the 'import substitution' literature. There is nothing on the implicit, or effective, rate of protection; the type of industry (consumer, intermediate, or capital goods) in which import substitution is occurring; the import intensity, or net foreign exchange saving aspects of the process; or the generation of saving by the new domestic industries (to name a few of the more obvious omissions). It is much more traditional in approach, but it deals with relatively simple and easy-to-measure concepts. In addition, if industries chosen for protection were to meet the 'success' criteria by entering Phase IV (full competitiveness with imports, or ability to export and earn foreign exchange), the country would not be likely to get into the kinds of difficulties that have sparked interest in the other aspects of the import substitution process.

3. ON NOMINAL AND EFFECTIVE SUBSIDIES TO DOMESTIC INDUSTRIES

The entire discussion of the preceding section was in terms of differences between domestic costs or prices and world prices. There is a rapidly growing body of literature which suggests that a more appropriate measure of protection or subsidy is one which not only measures the difference between domestic and world prices of output, but also examines and takes into consideration the prices of inputs into the industry. If one thinks of an implicit exchange rate as the equivalent of a nominal tariff (t_i) on any good, the language and notation of the measurement of effective tariff protection can be applied to the measurement of effective protection or subsidy from all sources. The emphasis of the notion of effective protection is on the protection given to the processing industry or the manufacturing activity.

The nominal tariff, t_i, represents simply the percentage by which the domestic price of an import would exceed its c.i.f. price, neglecting marketing margins and mark-ups. Nominal tariffs are usually studied in comparing tariff structures, since, from the point of view of a domestic import competing industry, t_i measures the percentage by which domestic costs of production could exceed the c.i.f. price of imports and still be competitive with imports. When there are domestic indirect taxes, t_{di}, however, domestic market price including taxes would still not be able to exceed c.i.f. price plus t_i, so that domestic producers could not have domestic costs that exceeded the net effect of the tariff minus the domestic indirect tax $(t_i - t_{di})$. If one were concerned with the differences between c.i.f. prices and domestic prices, one would be concerned with the structure of t_is. If, on the other hand, one were concerned with the incentives given to domestic production of import competing goods, one would concern oneself with the structure of nominal protection $(t_i - t_{di})$.

Recently there has been a substantial contribution to the theory of tariff protection introducing the notion of protection to a manufacturing process, or to value added, rather than to the product, or to gross value of output.[1] The basic notion is that the net protection to an activity should take account of both the higher price at which output can be sold and the higher prices that a producer may have to pay for his inputs. This measure of protection is highly sensitive to the share of value added and of non-tradeable goods in gross output.[2] Considering a product whose share of value added in gross output was 10 per cent (with no tariffs on inputs), value added could double in the industry with the imposition of a 10 per cent tariff. The 'implicit' or 'effective' rate of protection to the domestic producing activity would be 100 per cent. This relationship has been formalized by Johnson and by Balassa and in slightly different form by Soligo and Stern in their study of Pakistan's protective system, and I have sketched the general line of argument here.[3]

[1] Without getting into doctrinal disputes it is safe to say that Harry G. Johnson has done most to develop and spread an interest in this particular view of protection and its implications for trade, development and economic welfare. See: H. G. Johnson, 'Tariffs and Economic Development', *op. cit.* and 'The Theory of Tariff Structure with Special Reference to World Trade and Development', in *Trade and Development*, Geneva, 1965.

[2] This is discussed at length in my paper with S. E. Guisinger, 'Measuring Protection in a Developing Economy: The Case of Pakistan', *Journal of Political Economy*, October 1968.

[3] Johnson, *op. cit.*; Balassa, *op. cit.*; R. Soligo and J. J. Stern, 'Tariff Protection, Import Substitution, and Investment Efficiency', *Pakistan Development Review*, Summer, 1965.

If W_i is value added in industry i, X_i is gross output at market price, X_{ji} is the intermediate delivery from industry j to industry i, all at domestic prices, then:

$$W_i = X_i - \Sigma X_{ji} \tag{2.11}$$

in the absence of indirect taxes on output. On the assumption that tariffs and other indirect taxes are the only difference between world and domestic prices, one could compute value added at world prices by deflating all domestic flows by the appropriate tariff rate applicable to that good. If $\hat{W}_i$ is value added at 'world prices' and t_i and t_j are the nominal tariffs on products of industries i and j respectively, then:

$$\hat{W}_i = \frac{X_i}{1+t_i} - \sum_j \frac{X_{ji}}{1+t_j} \tag{2.12}$$

If we define T_i as the effective rate of protection, or the protection to value added in industry i, or the percentage by which actual value added exceeds that which would hold under 'free trade', then:

$$W_i = (1+T_i)\,\hat{W}_i, \tag{2.13}$$

or

$$T_i = \frac{W_i}{\hat{W}_i} - 1 \tag{2.14}$$

The statistic T_i has some unusual properties at its extremes. The numerical value of a related measure, U_i, which was used by Soligo and Stern, is more intuitively appealing for some ranges of effective protection. U_i is defined as the percentage of actual value added that is 'due to' the tariff protection, or

$$U_i = \frac{W_i - \hat{W}_i}{W_i} = 1 - \frac{\hat{W}_i}{W_i}. \tag{2.15}$$

The relationship between the two measures is:

$$U_i = \frac{T_i}{T_i+1} \tag{2.16}$$

or

$$T_i = \frac{U_i}{1-U_i} \tag{2.17}$$

The above formulations in (2.9) and (2.10) must be modified to take account of domestic taxes. Just as t_{di} can substantially change the incentive to domestic production expressed by t_i, so accounting for domestic indirect taxes can make a substantial difference in the effective protection to various industries. One can think of the problem in this way. Nominal tariffs raise the price at which a good would be sold in domestic markets above the free trade price and, in the absence of tariffs on inputs, raise the amount that could be paid to domestic producers. The domestic indirect tax rates then determine the share of the increased domestic expenditures on the good that will go (i) to factors of production (through value added) or (ii) to the government (through taxes). To take the simplest case, a tariff and a domestic tax of equal value would not change the value added in the industry at all, since they would completely offset each other.[1]

If one adds domestic indirect taxes T_{di} to the statement of flows, then domestic value added is written as:

$$W_i = X_i - T_{di} - \sum_j X_{ji} \qquad (2.11a)$$

Working on the assumption that tariffs are the principal determinant of domestic prices, and that indirect taxes on a tariff-protected industry would fall on producers of the protected good, value added at 'world' prices could be written:

$$W_i = \frac{X_i - T_{di}}{1 + t_i - t_{di}} - \sum_j \frac{X_{ji}}{1 + t_j}. \qquad (2.12a)$$

[1] This is a good point at which to bring up the host of simplifying assumptions that are made, implicitly or explicitly, in dealing with effective protection. Obviously, to the extent that the tariff raises the domestic prices, less will be consumed domestically, and so the industry would be discriminated against where tariff and domestic tax just offset one another. The entire exercise is partial in nature, as acknowledged by Johnson, *op. cit.*, and as emphasized strongly by R. I. McKinnon, 'Intermediate Products and Differential Tariffs: A Generalization of Lerner's Symmetry Theorem', *Quarterly Journal of Economics*, November 1966. One of the most important qualifications is that tariffs would change the exchange rate (assuming that it was in some sense an equilibrium rate to begin with) and that change would have repercussions in the domestic economy not acknowledged or accounted for in calculating effective rates of protection. There are other technical and economic problems, some of which are discussed by Balassa, *op. cit.*, and by Lewis and Guisinger, *op. cit.*

Except for the problem of whether statutory rates of tax, t_i and t_{di}, are equal to actual effective rates, it would be a matter of indifference whether one used output at market price and deflated by nominal tariffs, or output at factor cost $(X_i - T_{di})$ and deflated by nominal protection. In the calculations in Chapter VII, we deflated output at factor cost by nominal protection $(t_i - t_{di})$.

There are several uses to which the measures of effective rates of protection or subsidy can be put. One is to examine the nature of the incentive system as it applies to activities rather than to products. The structure of effective protection might be quite different from the structure of nominal protection and, thus, encourage activities different from those suggested by a measure of nominal tariffs alone. Another use to which the measures of effective protection can be put is to draw welfare judgments (of a partial nature) about the efficiency of a given set of economic policies. Thus, the U_i measure of effective protection to various industries, when aggregated over all industries, would give the share of value added in the sector 'due to' protection, or to distortions in the price structure. In order to apply a welfare interpretation to the calculations of effective protection, however, a rather long list of assumptions must be made, basically establishing that the industry is in long-run competitive equilibrium and that prices are equal to marginal costs. Calculations made using tariffs alone are undoubtedly not suited for drawing such welfare conclusions, since domestic prices seldom differ from world prices by exactly the amount of tariffs on the good. Some tariffs would be redundant due to cost reductions, others not effective constraints because of quantitative import controls, etc. Even if implicit exchange rates are used for both inputs and output, it is difficult to draw firm conclusions, since it is unlikely that one can observe any industry in long-run competitive equilibrium. The usefulness of the exercise of computing effective rates of protection or subsidy, then, lies in its power to combine the effects of price distorting policies on both output and inputs into an industry. As a result, such a measure may give a more complete assessment of the effects of economic policy on the incentives to draw resources into some activities and away from others. The empirical work in Chapter VI gives some estimates of effective tariff protection and uses the estimates as explanatory variables for the pattern of import substitution that emerged. In

Chapter VII, the results of another study that used effective rates of subsidy from all sources (i.e. used implicit exchange rates rather than tariffs to represent the differences between domestic and world prices) are discussed and are related to the welfare aspects of economic policies and industrialization in Pakistan.

4. ON DISTINGUISHING INDUSTRIES BY MAJOR USE OF PRODUCT

In the following chapters, I make a distinction among industries producing goods primarily for consumption, intermediate demand, and for investment and related purposes. The categories are pure neither conceptually nor empirically, since there are many industries that produce goods destined for all three uses. The distinction between goods by destination has assumed some importance in the literature on economic growth, and has played a role in critiques of Pakistan's industrial growth since Partition. For that reason, the categories are used in the empirical sections below.

Why should one make distinctions among goods on the basis of product use? The most highly developed argument based on these categories is that of John Power, who first applied it to the Pakistan experience.[1] The essentials of the argument are as follows. A country beginning with virtually no productive capacity in manufacturing, and facing present or potential balance of payments problems, will be tempted to follow a policy of placing restrictions on the imports of non-essential goods, usually consumer goods, for two reasons. First, given the scarcity of foreign exchange, it feels that essential needs of established industries, or potential industries, should have priority. Second, there is some appeal to the idea that restricting the flow of imported consumer goods will release more resources for saving, since consumption would be restricted by lack of physical availability. The difficulty with this approach, as has been noted by numerous writers, is that it encourages the domestic production of consumer goods only, and it does so both because there is a relatively protected market for consumer goods and there is a relatively cheap source of imported capital goods and raw materials on which to base

[1] J. H. Power, 'Industrialization in Pakistan: A Case of Frustrated Take-off?' *Pakistan Development Review*, Summer 1963.

the production of the consumer goods. Industries are established which have heavy dependence on imported supplies, and there is little incentive to develop local capital goods and intermediate goods industries to serve them. In addition, since this sort of policy is usually a concomitant of maintaining an overvalued currency, the export of the newly produced consumer-oriented goods is discouraged; domestic resources are valued more highly in saving than in earning foreign exchange. As a result, after the process has gone on for some time, the country finds itself with productive capacity heavily dependent on imported sources of supply and with no new means of earning foreign exchange. The argument that Pakistan had worked itself into this predicament by the early 1960s is made by Power, Khan and others, and a similar argument about Colombia is made by John Sheahan.[1]

The reason for separating products into the consumption, intermediate, and investment goods lines for purposes of the above analysis is two-fold. First, there is the thought that reduction in availability of consumer goods will encourage saving. Second, there is the bias in the incentive system that discourages the development of domestic industries. The backward linkages of the established industries all go abroad. As soon as the domestic production of the initial industry has begun, vested interests appear to maintain the cheap (because of currency overvaluation) sources of foreign supply. Those interests would actively oppose giving equal protection to domestic intermediate goods' producers, since such protection would cut into the profits of the consumer goods' producers.

In the chapters dealing with the more aggregative aspects of industrialization, I use a division of manufacturing industries classified by major use of product. In the later chapters, I examine the individual industries, the rationale for government policies, and the arguments about the consumer-goods bias of the industrialization policy.

[1] J. B. Sheahan, 'Imports, Investment and Growth: The Colombian Experience Since 1950', in G. F. Papanek (ed.), *Development Policy*, I, Cambridge, 1968.

CHAPTER III

Growth in Manufacturing and its Major Subsectors

As indicated in the introductory chapter, there were a variety of important influences on the pattern and rate of industrial growth in Pakistan in the period after Partition. One of the most important was the Partition itself. Even if Pakistan had not adopted a protectionist policy, but had attempted to trade freely with India, it is likely that much of the industrialization that occurred would have gone on anyway. The second important influence was the trade policy that was adopted. The policy had three major aspects: (i) overvaluation of the rupee relative to other currencies, (ii) use of quantitative controls on imports to regulate the level and the composition of imported goods, and (iii) a highly differentiated structure of tariffs on imports, and export taxes on the two principal agricultural exports: jute and cotton. The third major influence on the structure of industrial production was the domestic production of a variety of agricultural raw materials that could be processed within Pakistan instead of exported. While there is some overlap among these three forces, an attempt will be made to keep them separate for analytical purposes.

One of the most striking features of Pakistan's economy in the post-Partition period was the rapid change in industrial structure that took place, some principal features of which were given in Chapter I. The main characteristic of concern here is the high growth rate of manufacturing industry, particularly that portion of manufacturing known as large-scale manufacturing.

The industries analysed in this book cover virtually all the 'large-scale' industries included in the Census of Manufacturing Industries in Pakistan.[1] Four industries that were relatively large in the early

[1] 'Large-scale' industries employ more than twenty persons and use some form of mechanical power.

years of Pakistan's existence, but which have declined in importance, were omitted from the analysis: jute baling, cotton ginning, grain milling, and rice husking. All four processes are done partly in large- and partly in small-scale industry, and all four have extremely low ratios of value added to gross output. They are really more a part of the agricultural sector than of industry. Limiting the study to 'large-scale' industry does present a problem, since at least some of the growth in large-scale manufacturing is thought to have been due to a decline in small-scale industry over the same period. Thus, a part of what one observes is not growth of total industrial output, but the substitution of large-scale manufacturing output for small-scale output. Unfortunately, there is no way to adjust for this defect, since virtually nothing is known about small-scale industry in Pakistan, either in terms of composition of output, or the size of output, employment, value added, or the rate of change of any of these variables. The only thing that is generally agreed upon is that small-scale industry has not been growing as fast as large-scale industry, and that a number of manufacturing processes are carried out only in large-scale establishments. Since the entire analysis is carried on in terms of the large-scale sector, it does not cover everything, and the reader should be forewarned. Data problems are discussed in the Appendix, and detailed questions should be referred there.

Finally, all the data are in current prices. Since the analysis is concerned primarily with the differential growth and changes in positions among industries and industry groups, it is changes in relative prices that would be of concern. Relative price changes are discussed separately and explicitly, since they are closely related to understanding the industrial growth process.

Four years were chosen for the analysis of industrial growth, largely on the basis of data availability. 1951/52 is the first year for which one could get trade and output statistics with some degree of accuracy for a number of significant industries. 1954/55 (which is actually an average of the annual data for 1954 and 1955) was chosen as the earliest year for which good data could be obtained on the entire large-scale manufacturing sector. Censuses of Manufacturing Industries were taken in both years, and there is more certainty about export and particularly import data for these years than for earlier years. The data on production, imports and exports for 1959/60 are probably the best of any year in Pakistan, and that is the third year chosen. It is also the last year of the First Five-Year Plan, it serves as a benchmark for the revised national accounts, and it represents a water-shed period in economic policy-making in Pakistan as well. The final year chosen is 1963/64, on which considerable detailed work on production statistics was done by the Planning Commission.[1] Improvement of the basic industrial statistics in Pakistan is a continuing process, and even as this manuscript was being completed, further refinements were being made on data covering the 1960s. The changes that are being made, however, seem to reinforce, rather than contradict, the arguments made herein, and the more recent revisions of basic data have not been included in this analysis.

1. THE RAPID GROWTH OF MANUFACTURING INDUSTRY[2]

The differential growth rates among sectors of the Pakistan economy are given in Table 6. The sharp change in growth patterns between the 1950s is quite obvious. The change accompanied many shifts in economic policy and in the flow of resources between the two periods. Large-scale manufacturing, which was the most rapidly growing sector, was such a small part of total national product that even though it grew at an annual rate of over 16 per cent in the 1950s that growth was not enough to make any improvement in the level of *per capita* product in the country. The 1960s saw major shifts: agriculture finally began to make some headway (3·5 per cent per year), and the size of large-scale industry was such that it, too, began to have more effect on the growth of total product. The growth rate for the 1950s as a whole, however, hides a shift within the decade. From 1949/50 (a very small base indeed) to 1954/55 value added in large-scale manufacturing increased over 23 per cent per year, while in the next 5

[1] Details of the methods used in improving on published estimates, and the sources of data, are given in S. R. Lewis, Jr. and R. Soligo, 'Growth and Structural Change in Pakistan's Manufacturing Industry, 1954–1964', *Pakistan Development Review*, Spring, 1965. Some problems are discussed in the Appendix to this book.

[2] Parts of the next two sections are based on my article with R. Soligo, *op. cit.*

years the growth rate decelerated to 9·3 per cent. (Even that would be a source of envy to many countries, however.) The reasons for the deceleration are complex, but they are related (i) to an expected

TABLE 6. *Annual Growth Rate of Value Added in Pakistan by Major Sectors (factor cost of 1959/60)*

	1949/50–1959/60	*1959/60–1964/65*
Agriculture	1·2%	3·5%
Non-agriculture	4·1	7·3
(Large-scale manufacturing)	(16·3)[a]	(13·1)
GNP	2·4	5·3
GNP *per capita*	0	2·7

Source: T. M. Khan and A. Bergan, 'Measurement of Structural Change in the Pakistan Economy: A Review of the National Income Estimates, 1949/50 to 1963/64', *Pakistan Development Review*, Summer 1966.

[a] The growth rate from 1949/50 to 1954/55 was 23·6 per cent, while during the First Plan period, 1954/55–1959/60, it was only 9·3 per cent.

TABLE 7. *Annual Growth Rate of Value Added for Major Groups of Manufacturing Industries*

	1951/52–1954/55	*1954/55–1959/60*	*1959/60–1963/64*
Industries producing primarily:			
Consumption goods	43%	15·6%	12·8%
Intermediate goods	28	27	13·7
Investment and related goods	16·8	28	26
TOTAL	38%	19·5%	15·7%

Source: Computed from Appendix Tables.

Note: Data exclude four agricultural processing industries in all years. The period 1951/52–1954/55 includes only eleven industries producing about 70 per cent of value added in 1954/55.

slowing after the growth from the terribly small base had proceeded for a while, and (ii) to the shortage of imported capital goods, on which virtually all of Pakistan's manufacturing investment was based for the first decade of her existence.

As mentioned, data used here dealt with a slightly smaller universe than all of large-scale manufacturing, and data sources were slightly different from those used by the Central Statistical Office and by Khan and Bergan. Since the industries omitted were larger in the early years and were the more slowly growing industries, one should expect to find a convergence between growth rates reported here and those of the CSO. Such is the case, as can be seen from the data in Table 7. Data used in this study do not show the acceleration from the First to the Second Plan periods as do the National Accounts data, but rather show a progressive deceleration of the growth of total manufacturing industry. As is evident from the data on individual industries presented in Chapter VI, there is substantial variability in the growth rates among industries within any time period or over time.

An interesting change occurred in the general characteristics of the more rapidly growing industries over the three periods. Prior to 1954/55 the consumer goods industries were growing much more rapidly, while during the First Plan the intermediate and investment and related goods industries provided the most rapid growth. In the Second Plan period the investment and related goods industries grew at rates almost twice as fast as the rest of manufacturing industry. Investment goods industries were presumably those most affected by the import liberalization program in intermediate goods, as discussed below. While consumer goods industries did not grow as rapidly as other industries after the beginning of the First Plan, the former were certainly large in terms of their contribution to total value added. In most intermediate and investment goods industries, the rates of growth were very high throughout the period, and the lower growth rate for intermediate goods in the Second Plan period is due largely to the heavy weight of jute and leather industries, which primarily process agricultural raw materials for export. Had these two processing industries been omitted, the growth rate of the intermediate goods industries would have been about 20 per cent per year. Whatever one might say about the relative weights of the consumption, intermediate and investment and related goods industries, there was certainly no stagnation in the growth of the latter two groups. If there was imbalance in the structure of production due to a heavy weight of consumption goods in the late 1950s and early 1960s, one would have to look to the differential growth of the period prior to the First Five Year Plan for the explanation.[1]

2. 'SOURCES' OF GROWTH IN MANUFACTURING OUTPUT

Before looking at alternative explanations for the high overall rates of industrial growth, and for the differential rates within manufacturing, it is useful to examine the 'sources' of growth of various

TABLE 8. *Summary Sources of Output Growth by Sub-Groups of Industries, Aggregated from Individual Industry Statistics (percentage distribution for each group of industries)*

	Domestic Demand	*Export Growth*	*Import Substitution*
1951/52–1954/55			
Consumption goods	2·5	1·4	96·2
Intermediate goods	7·2	5·2	87·4
Investment and related goods	−6·7	0·9	106·0
Total 11 industries	2·4	1·8	96·6
1954/55–1959/60			
Consumption goods	55·7	16·5	27·8
Intermediate goods	34·0	57·9	8·1
Investment and related goods	71·8	1·0	27·2
Total 26 industries	53·1	24·0	22·9
1959/60–1963/64			
Consumption goods	110·0	−1·1	−8·9
Intermediate goods	47·6	21·8	30·6
Investment and related goods	108·5	1·2	−9·6
Total 26 industries	95·7	4·6	−0·3

Source: Appendix Tables. See text for definitions of 'sources' of growth.
Note: figures do not add to 100 per cent due to rounding.

industrial groups according to the scheme proposed in the last chapter: domestic demand, export demand, and import substitution.

Table 8 gives the summary results of applying expression 2.7 of Chapter II to individual industries and summing them for industry subgroups. Looking first at the figure for all industries there is a striking difference in the attribution of growth to the three 'sources'

[1] The arguments related to excessive investment in consumption goods industries are treated in Chapter VII.

in the three sub-periods. Virtually all of the growth from 1951/52 to 1954/55 was 'due to' import substitution, while none was attributable to import substitution during the Second Plan. The reverse is true for growth due to domestic demand: increased domestic absorption was not a source of industrial growth up to 1954/55, but was dominant after 1960. In the First Plan period, import substitution accounted for over one-fifth of growth of manufacturing output, while exports were responsible for about one-quarter. The data for the 1951/52–1954/55 period, of course, only cover some of manufacturing industry (accounting for about three-fourths of value added by 1954/55), so that the growth attribution is not accurate for all industry in the early period. As an order of magnitude, however, it is probably a good approximation.

To understand the differences among time periods, one should recall that imports contracted sharply following the collapse of export earnings at the end of the Korean War boom. In fact, imports as a ratio to GNP reached a peak in 1951/52 that was not repeated until well into the Second Plan period.[1] Some industrial goods showed a decline in total supply from 1951/52 to 1954/55 due to the sharp drop in imports. Thus, 'import substitution' in the early period was in part due to a movement towards high protection of domestic manufacturing industries. The absolute amount of imports fell sharply, corresponding to Phase II of the import substitution process outlined in Chapter II. Conversely, the lack of overall

[1] Imports and exports, in million rupees, for the period 1948/9–1954/55 are as follows:

Year	*Imports*	*Exports*
1948/49	1,459	958
1949/50	1,297	1,194
1950/51	1,620	2,554
1951/52	2,237	2,009
1952/53	1,384	1,150
1953/54	1,118	1,286
1954/55	1,103	1,223

It is likely that imports and particularly exports are understated for the first 2 years, due to unrecorded movements of goods between India and Pakistan. In any case, the decline in imports after 1951/52 is quite obvious.

Source: Pakistan, Ministry of Finance, *Economic Survey 1963/64*, Rawalpindi, 1954, Statistical Section, p. 56.

'import substitution' in the Second Plan period can be explained by the sharp acceleration in imports due primarily to increased aid during the period. Manufacturing output grew at over 15 per cent per year, but there was no import substitution since imports increased even more rapidly. During the First Plan, there was a moderate increase in the ratio of imports to GNP, and import substitution was an important 'source' of industrial growth.[1]

The pattern of growth attribution differs among industries in the last two periods. In the Pre-Plan period, there is considerable uniformity among industries due largely to the sharp contraction of imports. In the First Plan period, 1955–60, import substitution was equally important as a 'source' of growth to both the consumption goods and the investment and related goods industries, but was considerably less important in intermediate goods. Export demand 'led' in intermediate goods (due to the growth of jute textiles), and exports provided a market for about one-sixth of the increase in consumption goods industries' production. The pattern is completely different in the Second Plan period, with considerable import substitution in intermediate goods industries (particularly petroleum refining, chemicals, and paper manufacturing). Export growth continued to be important in intermediate goods. The growth of domestic demand for consumption goods (due to a much faster rate of growth of GNP) and for investment goods (as the rate of investment rose from about 10 to about 18 per cent of GNP) dominated these two types of industries, and both 'import substitution' and exports suffered (by the definition chosen). Exports would have suffered by any reasonable definition, since the absolute value of cotton textile exports and tea exports fell over the period, as domestic demand grew more rapidly than domestic supplies.[2]

[1] The relevant ratios of imports to GNP are:

1951/52	*1954/55*	*1959/60*	*1963/64*
9·9%	5·4%	7·7%	10·7%

The data are taken from Table 3 of this monograph.

[2] See S. R. Lewis, Jr., 'Domestic Resources and Fiscal Policy in Pakistan's Second and Third Plans', *Pakistan Development Review*, Autumn 1965, for discussion of this point. The cotton textile export figures rose in 1964/65, but they were depressed for most of the Second Plan period.

It is true that the greatest opportunities for further 'import substitution', in the proportionality sense, exist in intermediate and investment goods producing industries. It is incorrect to say that there was not significant import substitution in those industries through the period under study. In fact, the rapid growth rates of many of these industries was due to 'import substitution' to a significant extent.

The results of attributing growth in value added to various sources are summarized in Table 9, which has a format slightly different from Table 8. Table 9 divides the total growth in manufacturing value added both by industrial sub-group and by source, so the contribution of the particular 'source' in any industrial group to total growth in value added can be easily ascertained. The pattern of changing relative importance of 'import substitution' and domestic demand expansion as sources of growth is again evident, and in approximately the same orders of magnitude as in the case of gross output. An interesting dimension is added in column (5), where total change in value added is attributed to the industrial sub-groups. The influence of the differential growth rates is obvious, as consumer goods industries become relatively less important contributors to growth, while investment and related goods industries became much more important. Indeed, about one-third of the growth in industrial value added in the Second Plan period was attributable to the industries producing primarily investment and related goods. The consumer goods industries contributed about 70 per cent to manufacturing value added in 1954/55, but accounted for just under half of the growth of value added since 1954/55. The importance of exports as a source of growth in manufacturing value added declined sharply from the First Plan to the Second Plan periods, as did 'import substitution'. Again, both of these movements are due to the acceleration in domestic demand for all types of goods with the increased incomes and investment activity during the Second Plan.

The pattern of growth in manufacturing industries is quite clear and quite striking from the above analysis. The difficult task is to interpret the results in terms of either some policy related variable or some other appropriate notion of the determinants of growth patterns.

TABLE 9. *'Sources' of Growth in Manufacturing Value Added (1951–64 percentage distribution in three periods)*

Percentage of total growth due to:	(1) *Domestic Demand*	(2) *Export Growth*	(3) *Import Substitution*	(4) *Value Added Coefficients*	(5) *Total Change*	(6) *Annual Rate of Growth of Value Added*
1951/52–1954/55						
Consumption goods	−6·2	0·2	85·0	—	78·9	43
Intermediate goods	0·8	0·7	12·6	—	14·1	28
Investment and related goods	0·1	0·0	6·8	—	7·0	16·8
All industries	−5·3	0·9	104·5	—	100·0	38·0
1954/55–1959/60						
Consumption goods	31·2	10·8	16·5	−5·8	52·6	15·6
Intermediate goods	8·7	15·3	2·2	0·5	26·7	27
Investment and related goods	12·5	0·2	5·6	2·4	20·7	28
All industries	52·3	26·2	24·3	−2·9	100·0	19·5
1959/60–1963/64						
Consumption goods	45·1	—	−1·1	3·4	47·4	12·8
Intermediate goods	10·8	6·1	6·0	−3·7	19·2	13·7
Investment and related goods	30·6	0·4	−2·7	5·2	33·5	26
All industries	86·5	6·4	2·1	5·0	100·0	15·7

Source: See Appendix Tables.

No growth is attributed to changed value added coefficients from 1951/52 to 1954/55 because no independent estimate of the proportion of value added in gross output existed for those years.

3. THE EFFECTS OF PARTITION AND THE 'ABNORMAL' INDUSTRIAL STRUCTURE

One of the principal causes of the rapid growth of manufacturing industry in Pakistan after Partition was the abnormally low amount of manufacturing activity in the country at the time of Partition.[1] The reasons for the original location of industrial activity within undivided India are well beyond the scope of this book. The fact was that there was very little modern manufacturing in the area that became Pakistan in 1947. Even in processing of jute, there was not a single jute mill in the country, despite the fact that East Pakistan was the world's largest jute-growing area. Manufactured consumer goods flowed into the area that became Pakistan in exchange for agricultural raw materials (primarily jute and cotton) and food-grains (wheat and rice). Much of this trade was with other parts of India.

The precise magnitude and composition of flows of goods between Pakistan and India before Partition is not known. Such data as exist for the major primary products (jute and cotton) have been compiled and analysed by M. Akhlaqur Rahman in his important study of the development of inter-wing trade in Pakistan.[2] Rahman also includes some very suggestive, if somewhat aggregative, data on trade in 1949, a year which is probably fairly representative of pre-Partition trade patterns. According to Rahman's estimate, over one-half of West Pakistan's, and 80 per cent of East Pakistan's, foreign trade in 1948/49 was with India. By 1951, the share for all Pakistan had fallen to 3 per cent. The separation from traditional markets was both rapid and substantial. About one-third of Pakistan's imports in 1949 came from India. Over 60 per cent of those imports from India were manufactures. Exports to India in 1949 constituted over 40 per cent of Pakistan's total exports. Raw jute and cotton accounted for about 65 per cent of exports to India.[3]

[1] The economic reasons why a 'typical' structure would occur, and some problems of interpreting empirically derived 'typical' structures are given in the next section.

[2] M. A. Rahman, *Partition, Integration, Economic Growth and Interregional Trade*, Karachi, 1963. See especially Chapter 4.

[3] Data on commodity trade with India cited by Rahman, *op. cit.*, p. 102, come from Government of India, *Statistical Abstract*, Vol. 11, Delhi, 1950, pp. 1694–1700.

Since by 1949 considerable disruption of trade flows between India and Pakistan had occurred, these figures underestimate the importance of trade between India and Pakistan before Partition.

It is exceedingly difficult to make a precise estimate of the amount of manufacturing capacity that Pakistan should have had, or that it would have had if it had existed as a separate colony of the British instead of being part of a larger colony. One approach is to define a 'normal' level of manufacturing activity with some degree of statistical accuracy or substantive content. Chenery's work[1] provides a measure with both of these attributes. He estimated regression equations on cross-country data in the 1950s to derive a 'typical' structure of production for the mid-1950s. The variables that were statistically significant in determining industrial structure in his analysis were (i) *per capita* income, and (ii) size of country (in terms of population). By inserting into his equations the relevant data for Pakistan, one can get an 'expected' structure of production for a country of Pakistan's size and income level. The economic meaning of the typical structure and of the determining variables are discussed below.

For the data in Chenery's original study, Pakistan showed a very large negative deviation from expected contribution of manufacturing value added to GNP. If there is some normative content to the regression equations, i.e., if there are some real economic reasons in terms of comparative costs including the effects of domestic market size, to expect a country to lie near the regression line for a 'typical' country, then a part of the rapid growth in manufacturing industry as a whole would be explainable as a working off of a cost–price disequilibrium that is reflected by the deviation from the regression line.

Chenery's recent work[2] provides an even more precise and meaningful estimate of 'normal' production patterns, measured by the ratio of value added in manufacturing to total GNP. Based on a

[1] H. B. Chenery, 'Patterns of Industrial Growth', *American Economic Review*, September 1960.

[2] H. B. Chenery and L. Taylor, 'Intercountry and Intertemporal Patterns of Industrial Growth', paper presented to United Nations Conference on long-term Economic Projections for the World Economy, Copenhagen, August 1966.

fifty-two country sample, covering from 9 to 14 years in each country, Chenery and Taylor estimated normal production patterns based on (i) *per capita* income, (ii) population, and (iii) a measure of resource base in the country. Pakistan in the early 1950s was considerably below the typical-pattern line for the share of manufacturing in GNP. Pakistan's growth also showed the greatest deviation

TABLE 10. *Proportion of Domestic Production in Total Supply of Manufactures*

	'Typical' Country	*Pakistan 1951/52*	*1954/55*
2000/2100/2200 Food, beverages and tobacco	0·962	0·415	0·778
2300 Textiles	0·868	0·129	0·786
2400 Footwear/clothing	0·977	n.a.	0·998
2500/2600 Wood products/furniture	0·938	n.a.	0·345
2700 Paper manufacturing	0·629	n.a.	0·494
2800 Printing and publishing	0·977	n.a.	0·910
2900 Leather manufacturing	0·933	n.a.	0·989
3000 Rubber manufacturing	0·852	0·254	0·409
3100/3200 Chemicals/petroleums/coal products	0·842	n.a.	0·176
3300 Non-metallic minerals	0·958	0·800	0·806
3400/3500 Basic metals and metal products	0·913	0·142	0·440
3600/3700 Machinery including electrical	0·169	n.a.	0·092
3800 Transport equipment	0·413	n.a.	0·140

Source: 'Typical Country' from Chenery, 'Patterns of Industrial Growth', *op. cit.* for imports, and United Nations, *op. cit.* for production, for a country of $75.00 *per capita* income and 100 million population. Pakistan data are from Appendix Tables.

above the predicted time-series elasticity of manufacturing output with respect to income. Even though Pakistan's manufacturing grew faster (relative to normal patterns for her income level) than any other country in the sample, she was, by the 1960s, not quite at the share of manufacturing in GNP that would be predicted for her on the basis of population, resource base, and income *per capita.*

The original Chenery study and one of its successors[1] give a much

[1] United Nations, *A Study of Industrial Growth*, New York, 1963.

more disaggregated picture of industrial structure for 'typical' countries. Regression equations were estimated on manufacturing output and imports of manufactures, largely at the two-digit level of industrial classification, with *per capita* income and population as the independent variables. By combining the estimates for the two sets of equations one can get an estimate of the 'typical' or 'normal' share of domestic production in total supply for various industries for a country of specified population and *per capita* income. Such estimates are given in Table 10 for a 'typical' country of *per capita* income of $75 and a population of 100 million, which broadly represents the position of Pakistan around 1960.[1] The actual ratios for the same industrial groups in Pakistan for the first 2 years of our study are also shown in Table 10.

The striking characteristic of Table 10 is that for eleven of thirteen industries in 1954/55 the actual ratios of production to total supply in Pakistan were lower (in many cases considerably lower) than the ratios one would 'expect' from a country of Pakistan's size and income level. If the data available in a few industries for 1951/52 are suggestive of the situation in the rest of the industries, the extent by which Pakistan's manufacturing output was below a 'typical' level is even greater. This type of indirect evidence is consistent with the view that Pakistan came into being with a disequilibrium in her domestic productive structure and that a substantial part of the 'growth' that occurred after Partition was an adjustment process, working off the effects of a very large shock to the economy's cost, price, and productive structure.

A 'typical' structure of production based only on country size and income level is a concept some economists find difficult to accept. There is more direct evidence, however, on what the structure of production might have been if Pakistan had existed as a separate entity before Partition. J. Ahmad has recently estimated the importance of production in total supply of manufactures for a number of

[1] There was little if any growth in *per capita* income in the decade prior to 1960, though there was population growth. The 'typical' country is given to represent orders of magnitude that one might expect to find. Such low income and such a high population are unusual and the error in the equations at these extremes would prevent any precise statement even if one felt safe on purely conceptual grounds.

industries in India for a 15 year period.[1] Using his data for the early years after Partition, Table 11 compares India and Pakistan with respect to the importance of production and imports as sources of manufactured goods. It is quite clear that Pakistan was well behind India in the early 1950s with respect to the share of production in total supply of manufactures, particularly in the output of consumption goods and intermediate goods industries. By 1955, Pakistan had made rapid strides in approaching the Indian productive structure, particularly in those latter two groups of industries.

TABLE 11. *Domestic Production as a Percentage of Total Supply of Manufactures: India and Pakistan*

	Pakistan		*India*	
	1951/52[a]	*1954/55*	*1950/51*	*1955/56*
Industries producing primarily:				
Consumption goods	22·5	76·9	90	89
Intermediate goods	26·7	47·6	83	84
Investment and related goods	23·7	28·2	47	49

Source: Pakistan data from Table 7. Indian data computed from J. Ahmad, *op. cit.*

[a] Data for 1951/52 in Pakistan are based on eleven important manufacturing industries. See Appendix for details.

As was the case with the 'typical' country structure, there is no immutable law that Pakistan and India should have had similar productive structures. One should expect India to have higher shares of production in total supply in all industries, because of (i) the much larger size of her domestic market, and (ii) the significance of country size in determining imports and production of manufactured goods, as established by Chenery and others. Pakistan is a large country, however, and had markets of considerable size for a wide variety of manufactures. Differences in resource endowments between the two countries might explain the larger share of production in India.

[1] J. Ahmad, *Import Substitution and Structural Change in Indian Manufacturing Industry*, Memorandum No. 17, Project for Quantitative Research in Economic Development, Harvard University, Cambridge, Mass., 1966.

One must remember, however, that the most important imported manufactured good in Pakistan was cotton textiles, which was produced from Pakistani cotton in India and shipped back to Pakistan. Unless one were convinced of the innate superiority of Indian over Pakistani technology or ability, one would expect to find some of these goods produced in Pakistan after the two countries became separate. Chapter VI deals with individual industries in greater detail, but the basic conclusion there is that Pakistan had much lower ratios of imports to total supply in all industries than did India in the early 1950s. Many of the imports competing with Pakistan's industry came from India. All of this evidence points to the conclusion that, (i) by whatever measure one chooses, Pakistan was underindustrialized at Partition, and (ii) some part of the growth of manufacturing output was a readjustment to changed static conditions of relative costs due to the fact of Partition. A substantial part of the change in static conditions was due to the hostility with which India and Pakistan viewed one another, which made the continuation of a modified customs union unfeasible.

4. THE ECONOMICS OF A 'TYPICAL' INDUSTRIAL STRUCTURE

The notion of a 'typical' structure of production is important to the argument of this book and deserves some further elaboration. The basic notion of systematic relationships between economic structure and growth lies behind a great deal of research on economic growth. Chenery's widely read and influential article 'Patterns of Industrial Growth' gives a simple and readily usable means of predicting a country's economic structure. One interesting characteristic of Chenery's investigations is that the level of *per capita* income and the size of the domestic market (for which population is a proxy variable) are closely related to the level of production and competing imports of two-digit manufacturing industries.[1] The relationships hold over a wide range of countries with different natural resource endowments. The implication is that the comparative advantage of countries in producing various goods changes systematically as the

[1] Chenery also reported that no other simple variable explained very much of the inter-country differences in industrial structure.

level of development (or *per capita* income) and the size of the market in the country change. Further, if a country's actual industrial structure is different from its 'predicted' structure, there must be something specific, such as economic policy or a special resource endowment, that keeps the country from reaching the typical structure. To the extent that differences of actual from predicted structure are explained by resource endowment, the country can be said to be following its comparative advantage. When economic policy or other domestic distortion enters the picture, however, the country's productive structure may differ from the predicted structure because policy prevents the production and import variables from reaching the levels they would have reached under free competitive conditions.

There are many reasons for the close association between *per capita* income and population size and the level of production and competing imports in manufacturing industries. To the extent that minimum efficient plant sizes vary among industries, the size of the domestic market for goods would be an important factor in determining the profitability of importing or producing domestically in different industries. As market size increases (which could be due either to rising population with constant *per capita* incomes, or to rising *per capita* incomes), industries that previously found costs too high to meet competition from imports in small domestic markets would begin to find it profitable to produce for the domestic market.[1] In smaller or in poorer countries, therefore, one would expect to find lower ratios of domestic production of goods to imports of similar goods.

Per capita income is also related to supply conditions in different industries, since factor qualities and relative factor supplies and prices tend to change systematically with economic development. Thus, for example, the relative cost of producing complex engineering products might be much lower in a medium income country than in

[1] In general, due to transport costs, c.i.f. prices of imports will be greater than f.o.b. prices of similar goods if they are to be exported competitively. For this reason, an industry might be able to compete efficiently with imports, but not be able to export to third countries. Thus, the presence of potential export markets does not increase effective market size unless the world price f.o.b. for exports is above the low point on domestic average cost curves.

a low income country because of the greater supply, in the former, of skilled technicians and engineers, and physical capital, relative to less-skilled labour. There are, therefore, real economic reasons behind the very simple relationships Chenery found. The reason for believing that Chenery's 'typical' country patterns of production and imports do have some normative significance is that *per capita* income and size of country are proxy variables for the more complex determinants of the level and position of cost curves in domestic industries relative to the costs of importing.

Suppose one has a country whose economic structure differs from the 'typical' or predicted structure for its level of *per capita* income and size. I have argued that under certain circumstances this represents a 'disequilibrium', in which forces are set up in the economy which tend to move the country towards the predicted, or equilibrium, structure. The disequilibrium is reflected in a divergence of actual profit rates from normal rates of return in various industries. The equilibrating mechanism works through the cost curves and profit rates of firms in various industries. A given level of *per capita* income and population implies a level of skills, relative factor prices, and size of domestic market. Given the values of these variables, the profitability of producing various goods domestically is determined, as soon as one knows the price at which imports can enter the country. If a country had been maintaining a high degree of protection, restricting trade and keeping prices of competing goods high, one would expect that country to have higher ratios of domestic production to imports of various manufactures because the prices of competing goods are higher. If trade barriers were lowered, then some firms would find their costs greater than the new set of product prices, they would be forced out of business, and the ratio of domestic production to imports would fall. This latter is a mechanism with which economists are familiar. The value of Chenery's studies is that they contribute to our knowledge of the position of the domestic cost curves relative to import price for various industries in countries of specified levels of income and market size.[1]

[1] Since countries generally have protective duties of some sort, Chenery's 'normal' pattern of industrial development also includes a 'normal' amount of protection by the average country. This fact means that the predicted structure of production includes somewhat higher ratios of

To the extent that the level of income and the size of the market imply a set of cost curves in various industries, divergences of actual from predicted economic structure could be expected to remove themselves *unless* (i) economic policy had been used consciously to create the differences that exist, or (ii) there are some real economic reasons for the divergence that are not covered by the two simple proxy variables. The most obvious case of the latter phenomenon would be the presence of a cheaply exportable natural resource (such as oil), which would in general make the real cost of imports into a country relatively low and would result in much lower ratios of domestic production to imports than would be predicted.

In the case of Pakistan, I have argued that the structure of production in 1947 was a disequilibrium one for a country of Pakistan's size and income level. Pakistan has a noticeable lack of natural resources, eliminating that as a possible explanation. The ratio of production to imports of manufacturers was very low because of the unity of Indian and Pakistani markets, and the presence in India of productive capacity serving both markets before Partition. After Partition, even if extra trade barriers had not been erected, the normal difficulties of currency conversion and trade over international boundaries would have raised the cost of importing Indian goods and raised the cost in India of importing Pakistani raw cotton and raw jute. As these movements occurred, the incentives to locate plants in Pakistan would have increased, since it became clear that it was easier and cheaper to produce and sell cloth in Lahore, rather than produce it in Bombay and ship it to Lahore. Since the countries were at similar levels of *per capita* income, and presumably had similar factor price ratios, one important factor in making domestic production possible in Pakistan was the relatively large market for many of the goods that had been imported from India. The nature of equilibrating mechanism was the change in the profitabilities of investing in different industries. If hostilities had not existed, the investment in Pakistan might have been made by those firms located in India but desiring to sell in the Pakistan market. If the trade policy adopted had not been so restrictive, the equilibration process would have

---

domestic production to imports in each industry than would be true in a situation of free trade.

taken much longer, since the profitability of investing in Pakistani manufacturing would not have been so high. Even in the absence of economic policies that encouraged domestic production, however, there would have been considerable growth of the manufacturing sector as it responded to the increased profitability created by Partition.

5. RELATIVE PRICE CHANGES SINCE PARTITION[1]

On the basis of (i) the trade-restricting policies and (ii) the differential growth rates of the two major sectors of the economy in the 1950s and 1960s, one should expect to find deteriorating terms of trade for agriculture in the early 1950s and improving terms of trade thereafter.

Imports into Pakistan in the late 1940s and early 1950s were largely manufactures, and exports were virtually all agricultural. Given these facts the trade-restricting policy followed after Partition, and particularly after the 1952 trade crisis, should have turned the terms of trade against the agricultural sector, by restricting the domestic availability of manufactures, and creating a relative glut of agricultural products. Indeed, by the mid-1960s, the official interpretation of the 'saving strategy' during the 1950s held that the terms of trade had been deliberately turned against agriculture and in favour of industry for the purpose of transferring income to the high-saving manufacturing sector.[2] There is no evidence in public documents written when the policies were adopted, however, that anyone had such a policy consciously in mind.

With the magnitude of changes in productive structure, and differential growth rates among sectors that existed in Pakistan after the trade restrictions, one would expect some further changes in relative prices to occur. Unless growth in demand for goods in each sector exactly matched growth in supply, the more rapidly growing sectors would have declining relative prices. In terms of the two-sector model of economic growth, the more rapid expansion of the

[1] This section is based on my monograph with S. Mushtaq Hussain, *Relative Price Changes and Industrialization in Pakistan, 1951–1954*, Karachi, 1967.

[2] See Pakistan, Planning Commission, *The Third Five Year Plan*, Karachi, June 1965, p. 7.

industrial sector than of the agricultural sector would lead to rising relative prices of agricultural products, or falling relative prices of manufactures. In terms of the model of import-substitution with infant industries presented in Chapter II, one would expect that those industries in which the expansion of domestic production exceeded

TABLE 12. *Domestic Terms of Trade for East and West Pakistan (3 Year Moving Averages, 1951/52–1963/64)*

	West Pakistan		*East Pakistan*	
	Manufacturing Sector	*Agricultural Sector*	*Manufacturing Sector*	*Agricultural Sector*
1951–54	108·62	97·39	126·86	77·09
1952–55	112·22	91·14	138·55	65·32
1953–56	116·42	87·36	144·81	62·83
1954–57	112·00	91·41	128·54	78·34
1955–58	107·77	96·03	108·67	90·11
1956–59	104·52	98·76	97·28	97·19
1957–60	102·60	99·43	99·65	94·93
1958–61	98·05	103·13	101·67	100·65
1959–62	95·32	106·39	105·53	102·14
1960–63	94·75	108·28	106·21	103·01
1961–64	96·06	107·84	104·36	100·46

Notes: For the manufacturing sector's terms of trade:
The weights for manufacturing prices are the values added in each industry in 1959/60 and the weights for agricultural prices are estimated purchases of agricultural goods by the non-agricultural sector in 1959/60.
For the agricultural sector's terms of trade:
The weights for agriculture prices are the gross output of each commodity in 1959/60, and the weights for manufactured goods are estimated purchases of manufactures by the agricultural sector in 1959/60.
Source: Lewis and Hussain, *op. cit.*

the growth of demand, and in which cost reductions could reasonably be expected, would have had falling prices. On both counts, then, one would expect the sort of differential growth that occurred in Pakistan to result in a movement of the terms of trade back in favour of agriculture.

The terms of trade indices presented here for the two sectors of the economy, agriculture and manufacturing industry, represent the net barter terms of trade for the sector in question, i.e., the wholesale prices of goods that the sector sells relative to the wholesale prices of the goods that it buys. All weights for the indices used

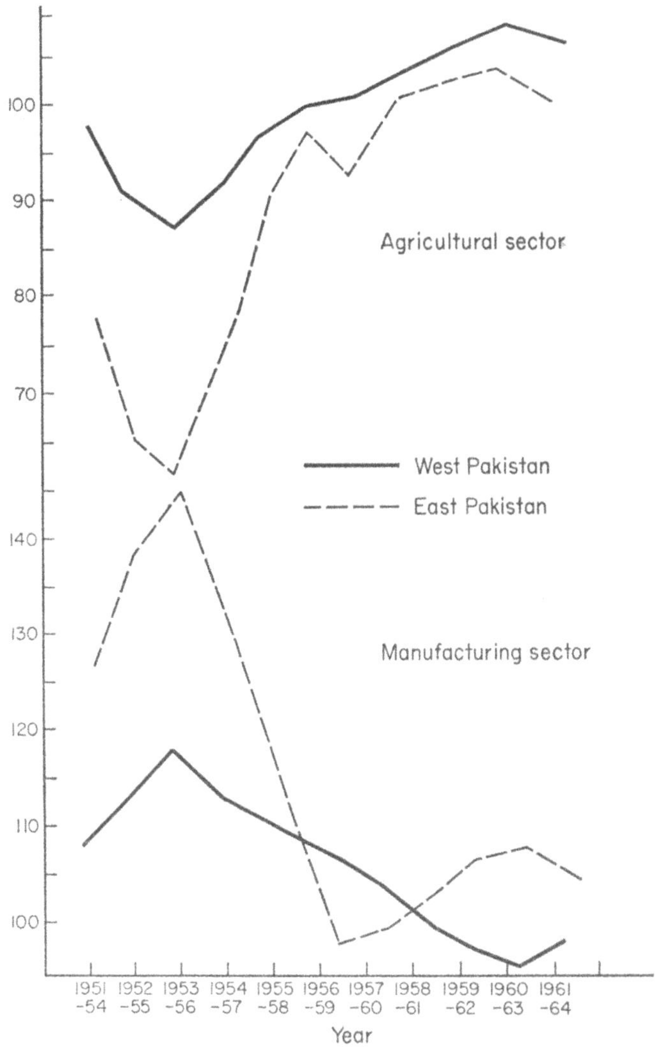

FIGURE 6. Domestic terms of trade: agriculture and manufacturing. (*Source:* Table 12)

here were based on estimated production, sales, and purchases for 1959/60, and all indices are representative of the movements of the relative prices of bundles of goods produced, bought, or sold in that year. There are many objections both of a practical and a theoretical nature that could be made about such a procedure. Fortunately, when the weighting schemes were varied quite considerably, the outcome of the analysis did not change.[1]

The principal results of the price investigations are given in Table 12 and are shown in Figure 6, where all numbers are 3-year moving averages. The net barter terms of trade of the manufacturing sector improved (and those of the agricultural sector deteriorated) from 1951/52 to about the mid-1950s, after which there was a reversal that lasted through the Second Plan period and the mid-1960s. The movements in East Pakistan were much sharper than the movements in West Pakistan, but in both cases the movements are quite distinct. The manufacturing sectors in both provinces faced worse terms of trade in the mid-1960s than even in the early 1950s, while the agricultural sectors in both provinces had better terms of trade in the mid-1960s than they had had before the terms of trade were turned against them during the 1950s. The movements are quite obvious in all cases, and they are of a considerable magnitude, particularly in East Pakistan. Farmers in East Pakistan had terms of trade in the 3 years 1961/62–1963/64 that were 60 per cent better than in the 3 years 1953/54–1955/56. In West Pakistan, comparing the same periods, farmers had terms of trade that were almost 25 per cent better in the later than in the earlier period.[2] As mentioned above, the use of different weights or different years changes the magnitudes of the movements somewhat, but does not change the pattern that emerges of (i) turning the terms of trade against agricul-

[1] Some of the variations that were tried are reported in the Appendices to Lewis and Hussain, *op. cit.*

[2] World prices and exchange earnings fell off in late 1952, but there had been substantial inventories of imported manufactured goods built up during the period of high exchange earnings, so that a sharp movement in the terms of trade occurred in the period 1952–54. In West Pakistan about 800,000 tons of wheat was imported in 1953–54, and both provinces showed fairly substantial harvest for that year, which contributed to relatively lower food prices in 1953/54. See Planning Commission, *Handbook of Agricultural Statistics*, Karachi, 1964, for data.

ture during the early 1950s and (ii) improving terms of trade for the agricultural sector from the mid-1950s to the mid-1960s.

The price data are presented on a provincial basis because of the unique structure of Pakistan's economy, with the two provinces separated by 1000 miles of land or 3000 miles over water. The provinces were kept almost as separate as two countries, and the structure of production, consumption and relative prices has been different in each. In terms of understanding industrial development in Pakistan, it is essential to keep several things in mind. First, there is less manufacturing capacity and value added in total and *per capita* in East than in West Pakistan.[1] Second, the level of *per capita* income is considerably lower in East Pakistan. Third, production of two principal fibre crops is quite concentrated, with jute grown in East Pakistan and cotton in West. The inter-wing trade that developed in the 1950s was such that East Pakistan became a net importer from West Pakistan, and the deficit was largely in terms of manufactured consumer goods, particularly cotton textiles.[2] That cotton textile production began first in West Pakistan is not unusual, since the raw cotton was grown in that province. The fact that the general trade restrictions of 1952 effectively cut off imports of manufactured consumer goods, however, had profoundly different effects on the two provinces. Consumer goods production, particularly in cotton textiles, had already begun in West Pakistan, so that the cut-back in imported supplies was met after only a short lag by (higher-priced) domestically produced goods. In East Pakistan, however, lack of both productive capacity and raw materials compounded the scarcity, and the supplies of consumer goods eased only after some time, as inter-wing trade provided goods produced in West Pakistan and as domestic production began in East Pakistan. The differential effects of policy in the two wings is a subject to which discussion returns continually.

Table 13 and Figure 7 give some indication of relative price

[1] East Pakistan produced about one-third of value added in manufacturing in the 1960s; and it received about one-third of the country's imports from abroad and one-third of fixed capital formation. *Per capita* product was approximately 20 per cent lower than in West Pakistan. See Khan and Bergan, *op. cit.*

[2] See Rahman, *op. cit.*, for more complete discussion of the inter-wing trade.

movements within the manufacturing sector. In both provinces, the prices of consumption goods relative to intermediate goods and investment and related goods were highest at the time of the restriction of international trade at the end of the Korean War boom.[1]

TABLE 13. *Intra-sectoral Terms of Trade for East and West Pakistan (3 Year Moving Average 1951/52–1963/64)*

	Consumption Goods Relative to Intermediate and Investment Goods	
	West Pakistan	*East Pakistan*
1951/53	108·08	125·99
1952/54	115·77	127·17
1953/55	113·45	124·03
1954/56	102·64	114·28
1955/57	97·91	110·06
1956/58	98·96	112·68
1957/59	100·86	110·62
1958/60	101·53	98·91
1959/61	101·28	90·24
1960/62	99·46	90·61
1961/63	95·99	96·82

Notes: Within the manufacturing sector, the weights for manufacturing prices are the gross value of output for consumption goods and for intermediate and investment goods.

Source: Lewis and Hussain, *op. cit.*

It appears that the consumption goods prices remained relatively high in East Pakistan longer than they did in the West, which is probably related to the time it took (i) to establish provincial production and (ii) to expand inter-wing trade.

Unfortunately, the prices of intermediate and investment and related goods are among the least reliable price data. There are substantial variations among the price indices for intermediate and investment and related goods industries in both provinces, depending on which weighting scheme is used (gross output, value added, net

[1] One should recall that at Partition Pakistan was more deficient in domestic production of consumption goods (relative either to the 'typical country' structure or to the Indian productive structure) than of other types of goods.

availability, or purchases by the agricultural sector). Such variation does not appear in the consumption goods prices, and they show a clear downward trend relative to either the rest of manufacturing or to agriculture after the early 1950s. It is clear that, to a large

FIGURE 7. Relative price changes within manufacturing: consumption goods prices divided by intermediate and investment goods prices. (*Source:* Table 13)

extent, the improved terms of trade of agriculture after the mid-1950s were due to the falling relative prices of manufactured consumption goods. Whether this was a good or a bad thing for future growth is a matter for consideration later. The main point here is that the group of industries in which import substitution had proceeded most rapidly in the early years experienced falling prices in the period following heavy import-substitution. Prices in these industries fell relative both to agriculture and to those manufacturing industries in which import substitution was still progressing. This may mean that the consumption goods industries had progressed out of the phase of high-cost domestic production while the intermediate and investment and related goods industries were either in the phase of unprotected domestic production (as was the case in agriculture) or the phase of high-cost domestic production behind high protection. In order to sort out the possible explanations it is necessary to look at the system of tariff and quota protection and the behaviour of domestic relative to international prices for manufactured and agricultural goods.

CHAPTER IV

Trade Policy and Incentives for Industrial Growth—I.

This chapter and the next present in some detail an outline of the trade policies adopted by the government of Pakistan in the 1950s and 1960s. The stated aims and the mechanics of the tariff and import licensing systems are examined, and the evidence on the functioning and the influence of these measures is explored, using as a framework the model of import substitution given in Chapter II. The basic aim is to quantify as much as possible the effects of the various trade policies and to relate them to the growth of manufacturing and its subsectors, as given in the preceding chapter.

1. THE STATED INDUSTRIAL POLICY OF THE GOVERNMENT OF PAKISTAN

One of the principal influences on the differential growth rates among sectors of Pakistan's economy was the lack of manufacturing capacity at the time of Partition. The second influence was the preoccupation of policymakers in the early years (and, indeed, in recent years as well) with domestic manufacturing industry as it related to the saving of foreign exchange. The earliest outline of official policy was the 'Statement of Industrial Policy' of April 2, 1948. It noted in part:

'The most striking feature of Pakistan's present economy is the marked contrast between its vast natural resources and its extreme industrial backwardness. A country producing nearly 75 per cent of the world's production of jute does not possess a single jute mill. There is an annual production of over 15 lac [1·5 million] bales of good quality cotton, but very few textile mills to utilize it. There is an abundant production of hides and skins, wool, sugarcane and tobacco—to name a few of the important products, Pakistan's considerable resources in minerals, petroleum and power remain as yet untapped. In laying down any policy of industrialization, note has to be taken of these deficiencies and handicaps, and a concerted effort made to overcome them.'[1]

The objective of the industrial policy was based on the evaluation contained in the above statement.

'Pakistan would therefore seek, in the first place, to manufacture in its own territories, the products of its raw materials, in particular jute, cotton, hides and skins, etc. for which there is an assured market whether at home or abroad. At the same time, to meet the requirements of the home market, efforts will be made to develop consumer-goods industries for which Pakistan is at present dependent on outside sources.'[2]

The last statement is the first mention of the 'emphasis' to be given to consumer goods industries. Other statements seem to indicate that the intent was to encourage any industry for which there was an adequate market within Pakistan. The 'Statement of Industrial Policy' added: 'Some of the heavy industries might have to come at a later stage of the industrial programme, but no opportunity should be lost to develop any heavy industry which is considered essential for the speedy achievement of a strong and balanced economy.'[3]

The next authoritative statement of industrial policy, indicating a slight change in emphasis away from consumer goods industries alone, came from the Economic Appraisal Committee which met in late 1952. Its final report was issued in February 1953. On the matter of priorities within industry it said:

'The main considerations that should govern the planning of industrial growth in the country are: (i) Use of our own raw materials, e.g. jute, cotton, bamboos, sugarcane, wool, hides and skins, cereal straws, oil seeds, limestone, gypsum, etc. (ii) Reduction of imports, particularly of essential items in which we should have certain minimum indigenous productive capacity. (iii) Maximum productivity in relation to the capital invested and maximum employment. (iv) Net social and economic advantage to the country.'[4]

[1] *Report of the Economic Appraisal Committee*, Karachi, 1963. Appendix No. 16, p. 50. [2] *Ibid.* [3] *Ibid.* [4] *Ibid.*, main text, p. 104

Economists will note which consideration lies in fourth place! Cotton and jute textiles, of course, received a full paragraph of their own. The Committee felt that other agricultural products produced domestically should also be processed domestically.[1] With the exception of requirements for cement production, however, minerals available in the country should not be utilized 'in the near future'. The Committee also went on to explain what it meant by 'essential items' in which domestic, rather than imported, supplies should be forthcoming. They were not all consumer goods.

'In this category would fall essential medicines and pharmaceutical products, insecticides and disinfectants, refined petroleum and other allied products, chemical fertilizers, certain heavy chemicals, *materials on which other industries are dependent*, and essential defence requirements. Likewise, light and medium engineering industries must find a place, as on them depends the future industrial progress of the country. . . . It may be added that plants to manufacture motor-trucks, cycles, light and heavy electrical equipment and machine tools would all come in the category of light and medium engineering industry.'[2]

On the methods which might be used to encourage investment in industries deemed desirable, the Committee was less clear. It definitely favoured tariff protection[3] (pp. 95–97), and was also in favour of a cascaded tariff structure, with lower tariffs on intermediate and capital goods than on final goods or more fully processed intermediate goods. It noted that the tax concessions to industry had been inadequate to the task of providing a faster rate of industrial growth, even though for 1952–53 the statement on concessions to industry noted that, 'No import duty is levied on capital goods and on industrial raw materials. . . .'[4] The Committee were apparently well aware of the additional protective effects of quantitative restrictions. In the chapter on industry they point out that: 'In

[1] It is interesting in light of more recent criticism of the sugar refining industry that the committee felt obliged to point out the 'cost of sugar production in Pakistan is at present much too high as compared with the production in other countries'. *Ibid.*, p. 104.

[2] *Ibid.*, p. 105, my emphasis.

[3] *Ibid.*, pp. 95–97.

[4] *Ibid.*, Appendix No. 17, p. 56.

normal circumstances the policy should be to give adequate [tariff] protection to indigenous goods after due investigation, and then let them compete with foreign manufactures, the import of which should not be restricted. . . . However, in the present foreign exchange situation, such a measure is not recommended.'[1]

In its conclusions about commercial policy and the balance of payments, the Committee acknowledged more market-oriented economic solutions to balance of payments difficulties but favoured quantitative controls and no change in the price of foreign exchange.

'Improvement in the balance of trade can be effected in two ways—by increase in exports and by reduction in imports. Reduction in imports is no real remedy, as it involves the imposition of controls, tends to raise prices of consumer goods, and reduces Government revenue. . . . Nevertheless, it is unavoidable in circumstances where exports are inflexible, and export prices are not favourable.'[2]

It is clear throughout the *Report* that the Committee had a general presumption in favour of tightest controls on imports of luxuries (in combination with high import duties), controls on other consumer goods, and relatively more availability of capital goods and industrial raw materials. In the industrial policy statement, however, they mentioned the need for domestic production of some items that usually would be classed as industrial raw materials and capital goods.

I think it is fair to say that the main emphasis of the Committee in regard to protective policy had two dimensions. First, produce anything that can be reasonably produced domestically. Second: once production has started domestically, ban imports of competing goods (in order to save foreign exchange). The *Report* states explicitly: 'In the case of items which are produced within Pakistan, the import should be banned or restricted according as the local production is sufficient to meet the entire or partial needs of the country.'[3] The only qualifying remark in direction of keeping down the cost of domestic production is that 'steps should be taken to attain proper standards in local production, [and] small imports of specialized articles might be allowed in order to introduce an element of com-

[1] *Report of the Economic Appraisal Committee*, Karachi, 1963, p. 97.
[2] *Ibid.*, p. 17. [3] *Ibid.*, pp. 18–19.

petition, e.g. simple lathes, scientific instruments, and laboratory equipment'.[1] The list of examples is significant, I think, in pointing to the Committee's willingness to entertain the notion of producing anything in Pakistan, regardless of whether it was primarily for consumption, industrial use, or for investment.

The broad outlines of government industrial and commercial policy aims in the period of early industrialization are fairly clear from the above statements. There was little in the way of systematic bias in the thinking at that time about favouring consumption goods production *per se*. The question that becomes important now is: to what extent were the general sentiments expressed in these documents translated into particular taxes and quantitative restrictions on imports?

2. THE STRUCTURE OF TARIFF PROTECTION

(written with Ghulam Mohammad Radhu)[2]

The rates of tariff on imported goods, classified according to a modified ECAFE scheme by type of commodity, are given in Table 14.[3] Several things are obvious from the Table. First, imports of consumer goods, and particularly luxury consumer goods and consumer durables, were discriminated against most strongly over the 9 year period covered, with tariffs exceeding 100 per cent. In the absence of offsetting domestic indirect taxes, domestic manufacture of such goods was presumably given the most encouragement. Second, the lowest rates of duty, less than 20 per cent, were given to imported machinery and equipment throughout the period. Third, there is some 'cascading' of the tariff structure, as Harry Johnson suggests is typical of most countries, where finished goods received the highest

[1] *Ibid.*, p. 19.

[2] The basic work on the structure of tariff protection in Pakistan was done by Ghulam Mohammad Radhu, and reported in his article, 'The Rate Structure of Indirect Taxes in Pakistan', *Pakistan Development Review*, Autumn, 1964. He has collaborated with me in updating his earlier work and in undertaking some new calculations of effective protection recorded here.

[3] While the data start from 1955/56 there were few significant changes between 1952 and 1955. Those that were made in that time served to differentiate the protective structure, so in 1952 it must have been more equal than in 1955.

TABLE 14. *Average Rate of Duty on Imported Goods by Types of Commodity*

Description	*1955/56*	*1956/57*	*1957/58*	*1958/59*	*1959/60*	*1960/61*	*1961/62*	*1962/63*	*1963/64*
Consumption Goods									
(a) Essentials	35	35	35	35	35	55	55	55	56
(b) Semi-luxuries	54	54	54	54	54	111	111	111	116
(c) Luxuries	99	99	99	99	99	140	140	140	142
Raw Materials for Consumption Goods									
(a) Unprocessed	26	26	26	26	26	27	27	27	30
(b) Processed	43	43	43	43	43	50	50	48	51
Raw Materials for Capital Goods									
(a) Unprocessed	23	23	23	23	23	28	28	28	31
(b) Processed	38	38	38	38	38	40	40	39	42
Capital Goods									
(a) Consumer durables	71	71	71	71	81	85	85	85	89
(b) Machinery and equipment	14	14	14	14	14	17	17	17	17

Source: Radhu, *op. cit.*, updated to include 1963/64 in unpublished typescript dated July 1965.

tariffs (50–100 per cent or more) followed by semi-finished intermediate goods (35–50 per cent) followed by unprocessed raw materials (25–30 per cent). Thus, one might expect the effective, or implicit, rates of protection to be higher than nominal rates on finished consumer goods, particularly luxury goods. Fourth, the extent of cascading, or differential tariff incentives, has risen markedly over the period 1955–1964. The tariff differentials (except for very low rates on machinery and equipment and high rates on luxuries) were not very sharp in the earlier years. After 1959/60 however, the differentials in the rate structure widened sharply as all rates increased, but the rates on consumer goods rose much more than those on semi-manufactures, and the rates on unprocessed raw materials rose least of all.[1] Imports of machinery and equipment were still relatively encouraged and their domestic production correspondingly discriminated against by the tariff structure.

If the average tariffs were any guide to the differential incentive structure during the early years of industrialization, the very high incentives for domestic production were given to those items for which the domestic market was the smallest: luxury consumer goods and consumer durables. Imports of these goods were most heavily penalized, primarily as a measure to save foreign exchange. Essential and semi-luxury (or semi-essential) consumer goods, which included most of the basic mass-consumption items (food, cloth, kerosene, matches, soap, etc.) received more protection than raw materials for production of such goods. Only since 1959/60, after the first rush of industrialization was over, were the differential incentives given to broad-based consumption goods (particularly semi-luxuries) widened sharply. It is true throughout, however, that producer durables had low tariffs, and, if the classification system is right, the duties on raw materials for producer durables exceeded the duties on the goods themselves.

While the average tariffs as given in Table 14 are of some interest, they are not the determinants of the level of protection. First, there are offsets to tariff protection in the form of domestic indirect

[1] The sharp increase in 1960/65 followed the recommendations of the Taxation Enquiry Commission, which submitted its Report in the Spring of 1960. 1960/61 was also the first fiscal year of the Second Five Year Plan period (1960–65).

taxes. In the extreme case, a tariff on imports accompanied by an indirect tax of the same amount on domestic production would result in no incentive to domestic production. When the rate of domestic indirect tax is subtracted from the tariff rate (including sales taxes on imported goods) we call the resulting measure the 'nominal protection', while we call the tariff rate alone the 'nominal tariff'. Second, using the input–output structure of the various

TABLE 15. *Average Rates of Tariff Protection on Major Groups of Manufacturing Industries, 1954/55 and 1963/64*

	Average Tariff		*Average Nominal Protection*		*Average Effective Protection*[b]	
	1954/55	*1963/64*	*1954/55*	*1963/64*	*1954/55*	*1963/64*
Industries producing primarily:						
Consumption goods	65	88	53	66	76	74
Intermediate goods	40	54	32	33	71	60
Investment and related goods	39	44	33	35	49	81[a]

[a] The very high average rate for investment and related goods industries in 1963/64 is due primarily to extreme value for transport equipment and metal products.

[b] The expression used for effective protection follows R. Soligo and J. J. Stern, 'Tariff Protection, Import Substitution, and Investment Efficiency', *Pakistan Development Review*, Summer 1965; and is to be interpreted as: 'the percentage of value added in the industry that is due to tariff protection'. If one wanted to use the usual measure (the percentage by which value added could exceed 'free trade' value added) the numerical value would be much higher.

Source: Table 32 of the present monograph, based on Radhu's earlier work, *op. cit.*, and the methods explained in the Appendix.

industries, one can compute the level of effective or implicit protection, or the protection to the value added in the industry, which basically takes into account both the tariffs on the inputs into the good and the tariff on the good itself. The methods were discussed in Chapter II. We computed all three measures of protection for the industries on which production and trade data were available. The results were averaged for the three groups of industries according to major use of product and are given in Table 15 for 1954/55 and for 1963/64.

Averages can be misleading, and these rates of protection are no exception. They hide a considerable amount of inter- and intra-industry variation that will become more evident in Chapter VI. Within each major group there are some industries with much higher, and some with much lower, rates of protection. The rates of nominal tariff and nominal protection increased over the decade, but not by so much as one might have expected from Table 14. Domestic indirect tax rates were also increased over the decade, offsetting part (and in some industries a large part) of the increased tariff protection. If one ignores the figure for effective protection of investment and related goods for 1963/64 (because of the distorting effects of the two industries mentioned in the Table) there is a clear increase in the differential protection given to the two groups of industries over the period covered. The investment and related goods industries were relatively more discriminated against, or relatively less protected, in the more recent period than in the early period.

The tariff structure was differentiated throughout, tending to favour domestic production of consumer goods over that of intermediates, and that of intermediates over the production of investment and related goods. It is also fairly clear, however, that the extent of differential tariff protection increased markedly over the period, and that there were relatively more equal incentives to the domestic production of different types of goods in the early period than there were in the later period.

3. THE IMPORT CONTROL SYSTEM IN PAKISTAN[1]

While the tariff structure played some role in directing resources in Pakistan, that role was a relatively minor one, as will be seen below. The principal determinant of the structure of imports and the set of domestic relative prices was the import licensing system. A brief

[1] Considerable research on the mechanics and the impact of the import licensing system has been undertaken by the staff of the P.I.D.E. This description of the system draws heavily on that work, particularly: S. N. H. Naqvi, 'Import Licensing in Pakistan', *Pakistan Development Review*, Spring 1964; and 'The Allocative Biases of Pakistan's Commercial Policy: 1953 to 1963', *Pakistan Development Review*, Winter, 1966; and P. S. Thomas, 'Import Licensing and Import Liberalization in Pakistan', *Pakistan Development Review*, Winter, 1966.

description of the system and its evolution is necessary, since its mechanics are an important aspect of its effect on prices and incentives.

From 1953 to 1964, virtually all imports into Pakistan were regulated by some form of quantitative controls. In the government and semi-government sectors, foreign exchange was allocated among various agencies, Ministries, and public corporations for 'development' and 'non-development' imports. In the private sector, detailed and comprehensive licensing controlled the level and the composition of imports, specifying the importer, the commodities he could import, and, in many cases, currency areas or countries from which the imports must come. It is with the private sector control system that most discussion has been concerned.[1]

Following the collapse of export earnings when the Korean War boom ended, Pakistan was forced into the position where, at existing exchange rates, demand for imported goods greatly exceeded those that could be provided from foreign exchange earnings and reserves. Of the possible alternative solutions, Pakistan chose to use quantitative restrictions on imports, and strict controls of foreign exchange transactions, and she chose not to change the official exchange rate. The latter policy was modified in 1955 when the official exchange rate was changed from its pre-Partition value of Rs. 3.30 per U.S. dollar to Rs. 4.75 per U.S. dollar, which put it on a par with the Indian rupee once again. Even this devaluation did not remove the disequilibrium in the balance of payments, however, and a situation of excess demand continued to exist. The first 6 month 'shipping period' under the new controls ran from January to June, 1953, and the 6-monthly announcement of import licensing policy was an

[1] Thomas, *op. cit.*, found that the value of licences issued averaged something under two-thirds of the value of 'private' imports as recorded by the CSO. This does not mean that one-third was not subject to restrictions, but simply that some other locus of rationing authority controlled their imports. These decision-making authorities are discussed by Thomas. Imports of the semi-public and 'autonomous' bodies which were regulated through government committees were classified by the CSO as 'private' sector imports. All quantitative statements about importance of various types of licences are based on Thomas's work. Private sector import licences were issued by the Chief Controller of Imports and Exports in the Ministry of Commerce.

important feature of economic and business life in Pakistan from 1953 to June of 1965. It should be emphasized that the system did in fact work, in the sense that it very effectively both limited the level and controlled the composition of imports.

An import licence in Pakistan is a permit to an individual or firm to import a specified value of a specified type of commodity (or group of commodities) into a specified part of the country. Licences are not legally transferable among individuals nor may they be used to import commodities other than those specified. From 1953 to 1965, the dominant types of licences were commercial licences (which were issued to importers who were generally expected to re-sell the commodities) and industrial licences (which were issued to manufacturers for machinery and equipment, spare parts, and raw materials, exclusively for their own use). In both cases, one licensing decision by the CCI&E determined simultaneously *who* could import *what* items worth *how much* into *which* geographic area. Such simultaneity was possible because each registered importer held an accounting unit of categories (for commercial importers) or quotas (for industrial importers) which specified in value terms the basic unit of each commodity, or commodity group, he could import. Since an importer had to be registered in a particular geographical area, the decision by the CCI&E on the percentage of the standard unit that would be allowed for each item for each category/quota holder also specified for total imports the geographic, commodity, and recipient distribution, and the shares that would be entering for (legal) resale.

Continuity in the system and orderliness in the method of allocation were added because there were only marginal changes each year in the persons who were category and quota holders. Registered category holders were primarily those firms who had imported during the 1950–52 period, and their categories (accounting units) in each commodity were determined by what they had actually imported in that period. Somewhat more flexibility was available for the industrial importers (or quota holders), since one could become a registered industrial importer and receive a quota *if* one's investment was properly sanctioned, i.e., if one had followed the appropriate procedures recognized by other agencies of the government. A quota is an 'entitlement', based essentially on installed capacity. Recommendations on the value of a firm's entitlement were made by the Ministry of Industries.[1] Licences for an original import of capital goods to install a new plant were granted on approval of some official agency, the specific agency depending in part on the source of finance. Once capacity was installed, the quota holders from past years became claimants on foreign exchange resources.

In determining the allocation to each importer and each type of good, there were several criteria in use, most of which were thought of in terms of 'essentiality' to the economy. 'Essentiality' was a broad heading used to include decisions about, e.g., regional distribution, luxury or non-luxury imports, or exchange-earning or exchange-saving nature of the activity receiving the imports. There was some formal and some informal coordination between taxing and licensing authorities, but not a great deal. There was general agreement about what goods were luxuries and what were essentials, so that taxes were high and percentage of category low for silver-brocaded silk goods, Scotch whisky, and large passenger cars, and the reverse was true for non-fat dried milk and vital drugs. On the broad list of things in between, however, there was considerable room for differences of opinion. Quantity decisions by licensing authorities did not necessarily coincide with the price (or tax) decisions by tariff authorities. One important activity of the licensing authority was the power to ban imports of particular goods, sometimes in agreement with the Tariff Commission (which determined 'protective' as opposed to 'revenue' tariffs) and sometimes not. Licensing was used explicitly as a protective or exchange-saving device in these cases. On the exchange-earning side, special consideration was given to export industries, both through the Export Bonus Scheme (after 1959) and through the use of extra import licences for raw materials and spare parts (higher percentages of entitlement for 'export' industries).

The Export Bonus Scheme essentially introduced multiple exchange rates for some commodities. Exporters of certain goods received a transferable import licence (Bonus Voucher) equal to a fixed proportion (the rate of Bonus) of the f.o.b. value of exports.

[1] See the three summary volumes published by the Ministry of Industries *Report on the Survey of Requirements of Industries*, in Karachi (1957), and in East Pakistan, 1960, and in West Pakistan, 1960.

This licence could be sold on an organized market, usually at a substantially higher value than the face value of the licence. The Bonus Voucher could be used as an import licence for a specified list of commodities, which included a variety of items ranging from refrigerators and coffee percolators to lathes and industrial chemicals. The effective rate of exchange for exports on Bonus has varied from about 30 to 60 per cent above the official rate, while the effective rate for imports on Bonus has been 100 to 150 per cent above the official rate.[1]

The Export Bonus Scheme in 1959 began a much-heralded program of 'import liberalization' in Pakistan, which was extremely important in several ways. First, over the period 1959–64 total imports increased much more rapidly than exports or GNP, and the composition of imports continued to shift towards imports of capital goods and processed intermediate goods. Second, market forces were increasingly relied upon to determine the commodity composition of imports. Third, a variety of new devices were introduced into the licensing system to increase the flexibility of entrance into the import trade. These new devices were both (i) an integral part of the first two developments and (ii) a separate element for distributing more widely the windfall gains from being an import licensee. Fourth, there were substantial increases in the rates of duties on imported goods, which acted, from the cost side, to reduce the excess demand for imports.[2]

[1] The mechanics of the Bonus Scheme and an analysis of it are given in H. Bruton and S. R. Bose, *The Pakistan Export Bonus Scheme*, Karachi, 1963, and some of its effects are outlined by S. N. H. Naqvi, 'The Balance-of-Payments Problem and Resource Allocation in Pakistan', *Pakistan Development Review*, Autumn 1963. Substantial incentives have also been given to exporters through the use of import privileges in the form of additional import licences. These schemes are described in W. E. Hecox, *The Use of Import Privileges as Incentive to Exporters in Pakistan*, PIDE Research Report No. 30, Karachi, 1965, and a good summary description is given in Thomas, *op. cit.*, Naqvi, 'Allocative Biases', *op. cit.* and W. E. Hecox, *The Control and Composition of Commercial Imports in Pakistan*, unpublished M.A. Thesis, Syracuse University, 1967, have recently added a further quantitative dimension to knowledge about the licensing system.

[2] The liberalization program is discussed thoroughly in Thomas, *op. cit.* and Hecox, *Control and Composition*, *op. cit.*

Besides the Export Bonus Scheme, which allowed a free market in import licences (Bonus Vouchers) for certain commodities, there were three new schemes introduced into the licensing system in the early 1960s. First was an 'automatic' licensing system for both commercial and industrial importers. It allowed importers to get more than one licence for a commodity in one shipping period. The second development was a new Open General Licence (OGL) which was introduced in 1961. The main purpose of the new OGL was to allow newcomers into the import trade, particularly those from areas outside the major industrial and commercial centres. One of its principal effects was to give a wider distribution of the gains from possessing an import licence, but there was also a substantial amount of foreign exchange allocated to the new OGL importers. Finally, a major departure from quantitative controls was made in 1964, with the introduction of the 'Free List'. Initially the Free List was composed of four items which could be imported *without licences* by anyone who could meet requirements of credit-worthiness, character, citizenship, and who could import in appropriate sized lots. (There were minimum and maximum values that could be imported by any individual or firm.) The Free List was greatly expanded in mid-1964.

Despite the apparent freeing of the controls in the first three devices, it should be remembered, first, that each of these improvements was still a system of licensing, and direct controls were still exercised. Second, it would seem appropriate to think of these liberalization devices as a way of allocating the large increases in imports that became available (both through increased exports and increased aid flows) during the period of liberalization. Without increases in the level of imports, the liberalization would have been possible only by cutting back the allocations to established industrial and commercial importers. Such a cutback would have been most difficult both politically and institutionally.

The Combined Effects of Import Quotas and Tariffs on Import Prices

The tariff structure that evolved through the 1950s and 1960s became more and more differentiated and cascaded, and it provided increasingly high protection to domestic production of consumer goods. The quantitative import control system, however, was so detailed and so strictly regulated, that it either could have offset or could have reinforced the differential protection provided by tariffs, depending in part upon the degree of detailed coordination between licensing and tariff-setting authorities. A major empirical question, then, is the combined effects of the import control system and the tariff system on relative prices of imports and, therefore, on the incentives for import substitution in the various industries.

There are two principal ways of examining the effects of the import licensing system on the composition of imports and on the structure of incentives. First, one could look at the structure of licences issued for imports (classified by type of good or industry) examining both the composition of imports that compete with local production and the composition of industries to which licences were issued for raw materials and capital goods. Naqvi made the first analysis of the composition of import licences, and some relevant portions of his results are examined below. Unfortunately, there is no information currently available on the licences issued for the import of capital equipment by industrialists. This information, if available, would give a means of examining in detail the effects of government sanctions on the pattern of industrial growth.

The second method of examining the effects of the import licensing system is to look at the pattern of domestic relative prices that emerged as a result of licensing decisions. This method is used here. In the absence of quantitative controls on imports, prices of imported (and import competing) goods would be set by the c.i.f. price of imports, plus tariffs and other indirect taxes, plus a normal trade mark-up for the commodity. Differences between this price and the actual domestic market price could be attributed to the effects of the quantitative controls. Pal made the first comparisons of such prices in Pakistan in studies covering two periods close to the end of the Second Plan period,[1] after the import liberalization program had been under way for some time and just as the Free List was being introduced. An examination of his data and conclusions gives a fairly precise idea of the extent to which the licensing system affected

[1] M. L. Pal, 'The Determinants of the Domestic Prices of Imports', *Pakistan Development Review*, Winter 1964, 'Domestic Prices of Imports in Pakistan: Extension of Empirical Findings', *Pakistan Development Review*, Winter 1965.

the price structure even after the restrictions had been loosened.

The average mark-ups for the goods Pal surveyed are shown in Table 16. These figures represent unweighted averages of the percentage by which domestic wholesale prices exceeded full landed

TABLE 16. *Average Percentage Mark-ups and Implied Shadow Price of Foreign Exchange for Imports*

	Karachi 1964 Survey		*Karachi 1964/65 Survey*		*Chittagong 1964/65 Survey*
Consumption goods	61	(63)[a]	55	(60)[a]	51
Raw materials	57	(60)	39	(45)	40
Capital goods	62	(63)	37	(39)	38
Total	59	(61)	43	(48)	42
'Excess' mark-up[b]	47	(49)	31	(36)	30

[a] Numbers in parentheses indicate average mark-ups on those goods included in *both* Karachi Surveys.

[b] 'Normal' mark-up was taken as 12 per cent, as indicated in Pal's second article. The figure was arrived at through interviews and from evidence contained in Tariff Commission Reports. The 'excess' mark-up is an indication of the percentage by which import prices including duties would have to be raised to clear the market for imports.

Source: Computed from Tables in two articles by Pal, *op. cit.*

cost of imports. For the first survey in Karachi this figure was around 60 per cent, while for the second survey in Chittagong and Karachi, 6 months later, and for a larger and slightly different sample of goods, the average mark-up was between 40 and 45 per cent.[1] Table 16 also gives the average mark-ups for the forty-two goods common to both Karachi samples. The mark-up came to about 60 per cent in the first and between 45 and 50 per cent in the second. Broadly speaking, the domestic value of imports in Pakistan in the mid-1960's exceeded their full duty-paid value at the official exchange rate by approximately 50 per cent.

[1] When margins were weighted by the value of imports of the four-digit commodity groups represented by the goods in the survey for November 1964–January 1965, the average mark-up in East Pakistan remained at 42 per cent, while the average in West Pakistan rose to 56 per cent. Weighting makes some difference but does not change the orders of magnitude. See Pal, *op. cit.*, for details.

Pal's data can be used to examine in detail the relations among types of import licence (i.e. whether the good was nominally liberalized or not), types of commodities that were imported, and the levels of tariff on each, and to tie the analysis of tariffs to the effects of quantitative restrictions. The average rate of duty, mark-up, and price differential (the extent by which wholesale domestic price exceeds c.i.f. price at the official exchange rate), for major types of goods by type of licence are given in Tables 17 and 18 for Pal's two surveys.

In the first Karachi survey, the average mark-up was very similar for consumption goods, raw materials, and capital goods, and averaged around 60 per cent. Average duties differed considerably among types of goods, from over 100 per cent for consumption goods to only 23 per cent for capital goods. The price differential varied from 100 per cent for capital goods to 176 per cent for consumer goods. As the average mark-up above landed cost was the same for all groups, the duty was a smaller share o the total price differential in high-duty consumption goods than in low-duty capital goods. In such a case the use of average tariffs would not simply understate the extent of protection; rather, the extent of protection afforded to low-duty items would be systematically understated relative to protection on high-duty items. The low relative protection given by the duty structure to intermediate and capital goods, therefore, appears to have been offset to some extent by the licensing system, even in the mid-1960s.

There is another important implication of the figures in Table 17. The fact that the average mark-up on raw materials and capital goods was about 60 per cent means that the firm that did not receive import licences for the intermediate products it used paid 60 per cent more for its imported inputs than its competitors, who did receive licences. The impact of this price differential could have been felt in two ways. If input coefficients were fixed, and productivity among firms was constant, there was a considerable differential between profitabilities of firms receiving and those not receiving import licences.[1] Alternatively, if substitution was possible between

[1] If imports at landed cost are 15 per cent of gross output, value added is 30 per cent of gross output, and profits are one-third of value added, a firm that had to buy its imports domestically would have its profits

imported inputs and domestic inputs or primary factors, the very large differences in prices encouraged the use of imported goods by licensees who were being subsidized to a considerable extent by the licensing system. With an undervaluation of imported goods

TABLE 17. *Unweighted Averages of Duties, Mark-ups and Price Differentials, Karachi Survey, 1964*

Commodity Group	*Duty*	*Mark-up*	*Price Differential*
A. Consumption goods	109·3	60·7	176·2
B, C. Raw materials:			
1. Regular licence	47·0	64·4	159·5
2. OGL	33·5	57·7	115·9
3. Other licence	21·3	11·5	38·5
TOTAL raw materials	38·4	57·3	129·0
D. Capital goods	23·0	61·7	100·4
B, C, D. Raw materials and capital goods	34·5	58·4	121·5
ALL ITEMS	52·2	59·0	133·9

The average price differential for all goods of 134 per cent represents an implicit exchange rate between domestic wholesale prices in rupees and c.i.f. prices in dollars of Rs. 11.11 per U.S. dollar. The official exchange rate was Rs. 4.75.

Source: Computed from Tables I, II and III in Pal, first article, *op. cit.*

by one-third or more, a reasonable elasticity of substitution among inputs must have resulted in substantial economies on imported inputs by non-privileged firms. If the price of foreign exchange had been raised to the shadow price of imports for all firms (holding duties constant), there would have been sizeable saving of imported raw materials for the economy as a whole.[1]

[1] If imports were 20 per cent of gross output and their prices were raised by one-third, an elasticity of substitution of unity would induce a drop of the import coefficient from 0·20 to 0·14, and an elasticity of substitution of 0·5 would drop the import coefficient from 0·20 to 0·167.

reduced by 90 per cent if the mark-up on imported goods was 60 per cent. The coefficients chosen are typical for many industries in Pakistan.

There are only minor differences in Pal's first survey between the mark-ups on goods imported under different types of licences. The two items in the 'other licence' category were on automatic licence and Free List, and they show considerably lower duty and mark-up

TABLE 18. *Unweighted Average Duties, Mark-ups and Price Differentials for Imported Goods in Pakistan, 1964 (expressed in percentage terms)*

Commodity Group	*Type of Licence*	*Duty*	*Mark-ups*	*Price Differential*
All items	Licensed	63·4	53·5	160·0
	Free List	32·2	29·3	78·1
	All types	49·2	42·5	122·7
Raw materials	Licensed	45·7	50·9	125·4
	Free List	36·1	30·7	85·8
	All types	40·2	39·4	102·9
Capital goods	Licensed	42·3	53·7	124·1
	Free List	27·7	28·2	69·4
	All types	33·2	37·3	89·2
Consumption goods	All types	80·3	52·9	187·5

Note: Only two consumer goods of twenty-four surveyed were importable on the Free List. Their omission does not materially affect the results, but it does simplify the Table.
Source: Computed from Table VI in Pal, second article, *op. cit.*

than the other raw materials. There is no significant difference between the mark-ups on the OGL and regularly licensed raw materials, however, despite the fact that OGL licensing was supposed to imply greater availability of the goods, and, therefore, lower mark-ups. In fact, there was a greater difference in average duties than in average mark-ups for the two groups.

Differences of behaviour of mark-ups on goods imported under different types of licence are seen more vividly in the results of Pal's second and larger survey in Karachi and Chittagong, summarized in Table 18. Figures are shown for East Pakistan and West Pakistan separately and combined, for various combinations of goods and licences. The average duties, mark-ups, and price differentials hide considerable variations within categories, as one might suppose. There are, however, some interesting and significant results even at the aggregate level. For all goods on all types of licence, the price differential was about 122 per cent while the average duty was 49 per cent. Thus, the exchange rate implied by tariffs would be Rs. 7.08 per dollar while that implied by actual prices was 10.55 per dollar.

There were large differences between the mark-ups on consumer goods and those on raw materials and capital goods; mark-ups averaged 53, 39 and 37 per cent, respectively. Duties differed much more than mark-ups, averaging 80, 40, and 33 per cent on consumer goods, raw materials, and capital goods, respectively. A considerable amount of the differentials by type of good, however, was accounted for by the difference in type of licence under which the good was importable. Average mark-ups on *licensed* raw materials and capital goods were about the same as those on consumer goods, 51, 54, and 53 per cent, respectively). Duties, as usual, were much higher on consumer goods (80 per cent) than on raw materials and capital goods (46 and 42 per cent). Both duties and mark-ups were lower on Free List goods than on licensed imports of similar goods.

The Free List *did* have the effect of bringing mark-ups (and domestic prices) down. There was relatively little difference between average mark-ups on groups of licensed goods even with large differences in duties, while Free List goods of similar types with somewhat lower average duties had substantially lower mark-ups. The stringency of regular licensing still was an important factor affecting domestic relative prices, even though the introduction of the Free List led to prices closer to landed costs for goods on that list. Even for the Free List items, however, the presence of the 'abnormal' profit margins meant that price differentials and, therefore, the nominal protection provided by both tariffs and quantitative controls, were more than twice the level of duties.[1]

The principal conclusion drawn from Pal's empirical work is that the licensing system and other less formal quantitative controls on imports worked to improve greatly the competitive position of manufacturers of import-competing intermediate and capital goods,

[1] Thomas, *op. cit.*, has considerable discussions of the hidden quantitative restrictions on Free List imports.

relative to the incentives suggested by tariff rates alone. Pal's first survey results, before the Free List came into existence, indicated an almost systematic offset of tariff incentives by quantitative controls, as represented by mark-ups. After the introduction of the Free List, this relationship was no longer true since the government's policy explicitly was to make available all imports of certain items demanded at c.i.f. prices plus duties. If Pal's results for the pre-Free List period were true throughout the period of stringent licensing 1953–64 then the structure of incentives for domestic production of different kinds of goods as implied by the tariff structure not only understates the general level of protection but also misstates the *relative* degree of protection given to the different goods.

Another, and related, conclusion to be drawn from an analysis of Pal's data is the enormous advantage given to those industrial import licensees who were able to purchase imports at landed costs. Industrialists not receiving import licences had to purchase raw materials and spares at prevailing prices that averaged 40–60 per cent above the price paid by the industrial licence holder. Using Naqvi's classification of licensing data, discussed in the next chapter, commercial licences issued for raw materials and capital goods in 1963 were about one-third of the value of industrial licences issued for raw materials and spares. The share of industrialists purchasing raw materials domestically at high mark-ups was quite significant. This latter fact, too, indicates that the mark-ups were an important part of the incentive to domestic manufacture of intermediate and investment and related goods, since the mark-up does not reflect a narrow grey market for raw materials but emerges from a market in which a significant share of imported raw materials and capital goods are exchanged.

CHAPTER V

Trade Policy and Incentives for Industrial Growth—II

The results of the last two chapters give the following broad picture of industrial growth. Pakistan began in 1947 with very little manufacturing capacity. Manufacturing output grew at a very rapid rate relative to the other sectors of the economy or to manufacturing output in other countries. Import substitution was the major source of output growth in the 1950s, and was important in all industrial subgroups. Import substitution took place most rapidly in industries that produced mainly consumer goods. Following the trade crisis of 1952, the terms of trade turned sharply against agriculture, and in the years of rapid manufacturing growth following the trade crisis, the terms of trade turned back in favour of agriculture. The principal change in relative prices of manufactures was a fall in the relative price of consumer goods, in which import substitution had proceeded most rapidly. By the end of the 1950s, there were even exports from the consumer goods industries.

In terms of economic policy there seemed to be little bias of planners in the early 1960s in favour of last-stage consumer goods processing as a first step in import substitution. Consumer goods industries were not necessarily to be encouraged. Industries that were to be encouraged were those using domestically produced raw materials. Policy statements did emphasize the need for tight controls on foreign exchange expenditures, especially for 'non-essential' goods. The tariff structure that emerged, however, was somewhat biased towards encouraging the domestic production of consumer goods, and this bias increased over time. One should remember, however, that the major increases in differential tariff protection came after much of the import substitution had occurred. Finally, detailed information available for the mid-1960s shows that the import licensing system may have offset the differential effects of the tariffs, since for virtually all goods domestic demand exceeded supply at landed costs of imports. Domestic prices of imports were, at the margin, determined primarily by licensing decisions, not tariffs or c.i.f. costs. In this chapter, the effects of the import licensing system are examined over a longer time period, though not in as much detail as in the last chapter. In the final section of this chapter, other possible influences on industrial investment decisions and on the pattern of industrial growth are discussed.

1. SOME MEASURES OF THE INCENTIVES GIVEN BY QUANTITATIVE CONTROLS THROUGH TIME[1]

Unfortunately, since there are few systematic data available on the behaviour of prices of imported goods, or on the c.i.f. prices of similar goods, there is no way of reconstructing accurately the movements of mark-ups and, therefore, the level of nominal protection including quota protection, that was given to different industries in Pakistan at different points of time. An alternative method of projecting such levels back through time was developed, using the notion of implicit exchange rates. An implicit exchange rate, as explained in Chapter II, is a ratio between the domestic wholesale price in rupees and the international (c.i.f. or f.o.b.) price of the same item in dollars (or any other international medium of exchange). Any distortions affecting the free movement of goods whether in the form of import or export duties, indirect taxes or subsidies, quantitative restrictions, or multiple exchange rates, will cause the implicit exchange rates to vary among goods.

A few words on the method of calculation are necessary before turning to the results and implications of the analysis. Implicit exchange rates were calculated for all industries and agricultural commodities for which data could be obtained for 1963/64. Using the same weighting systems that were employed in calculating the domestic wholesale price indices reported in Chapter III, an average

[1] This section is a slightly revised version of my article 'Effects of Trade Policy on Domestic Relative Prices: Pakistan, 1951–1964', *American Economic Review*, March 1968, and is used here with permission of the editor.

implicit exchange rate could be obtained for manufacturing, for agriculture, and for the subsectors of each, for that year. The average rate represented the domestic value of $1.00 worth of the commodity or bundle of commodities in question. As explained in Chapter II, this information is used to examine the difference between the terms of trade that agriculture and manufacturing did have domestically and the terms of trade they might have had if they had traded in international markets without the distortions introduced by the country's trade policies. The goods included were those imported and those exported, as well as, where possible, those neither imported nor exported, but which were tradeable goods if the proper set of domestic and world prices and exchange rates could be found.

In order to determine the movement in the implicit exchange rates over time, domestic price indices for each commodity or commodity group were used to project back the movements in the domestic price portion, and 'international' price indices were used to project back the dollar portion of the exchange rate. The 'international' indices used actual prices for agricultural goods. For the most part, export unit value indices of the commodities from major exporting countries were used for the manufacturing goods. The movement in the international prices was not so great as the movement in the domestic prices, and it was generally in the *opposite* direction from the domestic movements.[1]

Differences in Implicit Exchange Rates Between Sectors and Over Time

The basic results of the computations of implicit exchange rates for manufacturing and agricultural goods in East and West Pakistan and their movements from 1951 to 1964 are given in Table 19 and are shown in Figures 8 and 9. Figure 8 gives a picture from the point of view of the agricultural sector, where agricultural exchange rates are weighted by marketings, and manufacturing exchange rates are

[1] For this reason, one would have to argue that the *direction* of movement, not just the magnitude of change, was misrepresented by the international indices used in order to modify greatly the results presented below. It is not likely that such a large amount of distortion existed.

TABLE 19. *Implicit Exchange Rates for Agricultural and Manufactured Goods, East and West Pakistan (three-year averages)*

	EAST PAKISTAN				WEST PAKISTAN				
	Manufactured Goods		*Agricultural Goods*		*Manufactured Goods*		*Agricultural Goods*		
	Gross Output	*Purchased by Agriculture*	*Marketings*	*Purchased by Manufacturing*	*Gross Output*	*Purchased by Agriculture*	*Marketings*	*Purchased by Manufacturing*	*Official Exchange Rate*
1951–54	6·15	9·07	2·87	3·32	7·07	8·39	3·81	4·13	3·31
1952–55	6·62	9·74	2·73	3·01	7·63	8·94	3·81	4·15	3·31
1953–56	6·88	10·17	2·86	2·97	7·84	9·00	3·76	4·06	3·78
1954–57	7·00	9·81	3·70	3·77	7·66	8·51	3·94	4·19	4·27
1955–58	7·20	9·83	4·46	4·57	7·90	8·56	4·33	4·57	4·75
1956–59	7·14	9·46	4·85	5·01	7·96	8·57	4·73	5·06	4·75
1957–60	7·20	9·07	4·65	4·95	7·95	8·68	4·85	5·30	4·75
1958–61	7·21	8·56	4·75	5·10	7·73	8·59	5·06	5·60	4·75
1959–62	7·13	8·42	4·83	5·17	7·68	8·61	5·19	5·70	4·75
1960–63	6·85	8·29	4·87	5·09	7·53	8·41	5·40	5·79	4·75
1961–64	6·63	8·15	4·77	4·93	7·39	8·33	5·35	5·69	4·75

Source: Lewis, *op. cit.*

weighted by estimated purchases of manufactured goods by the agricultural sector.[1]

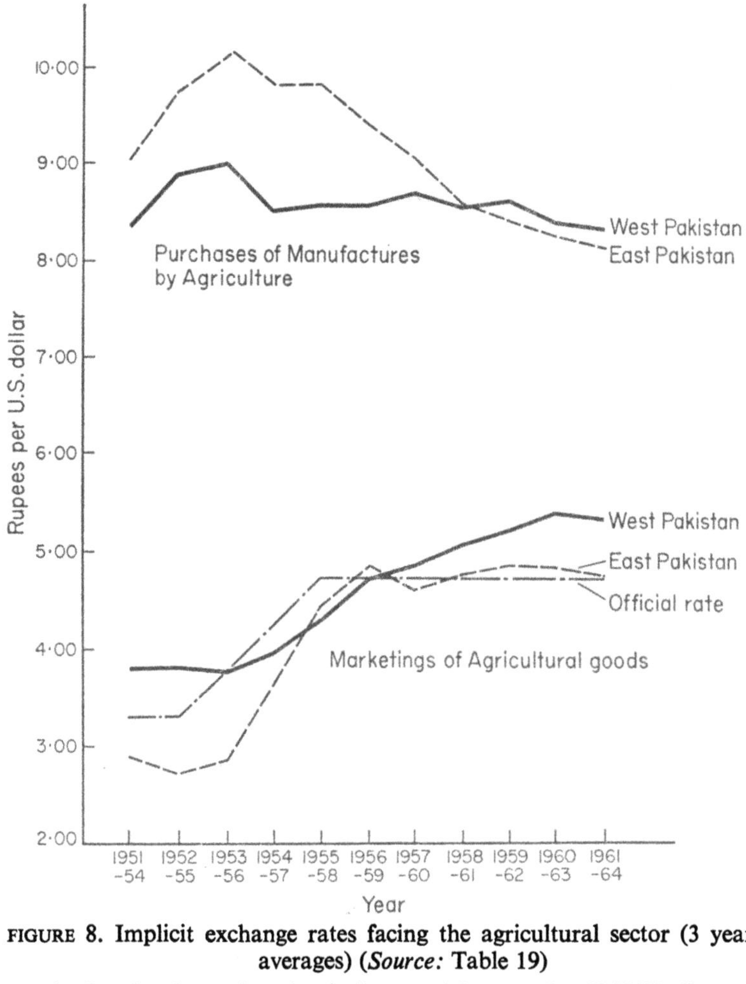

FIGURE 8. Implicit exchange rates facing the agricultural sector (3 year averages) (*Source:* Table 19)

[1] As for the domestic price indices, weights are for 1959/60. Several alternative estimates of purchases of manufactures by agriculture were tried, but fortunately the results were quite insensitive to the alternative weightings. The weightings and variations in weights are given in S. R. Lewis, Jr. and S. M. Hussain, *Relative Price Changes and Industrialization in Pakistan: 1951-1964*, Karachi, 1967.

There are two separate aspects of the behaviour of the implicit exchange rates for the two sectors. First, their relative levels give some indication of the extent to which trade-restricting policies on

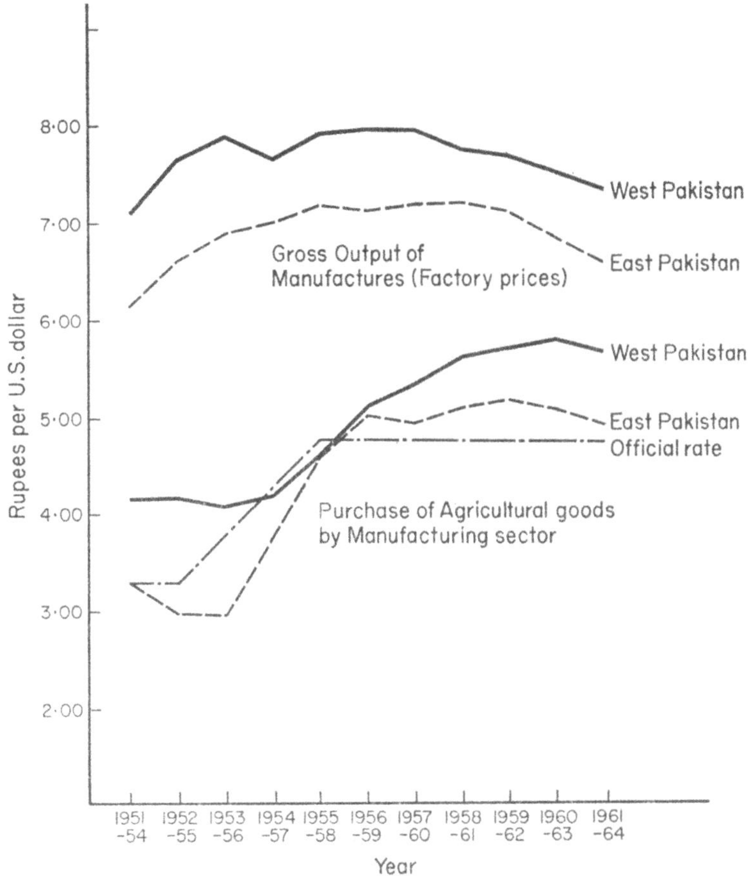

FIGURE 9. Implicit exchange rates facing the manufacturing sector (3 year averages) (*Source:* Table 19)

the part of the government had discriminated in favour of one sector and against the other. Second, the movement of the differential in rates over time gives some additional information on the extent to which the protected industries have moved towards reducing the cost of protection by lowering their relative implicit exchange rates.

Several characteristics of Figure 8 stand out. First, even in the mid-1960s the agricultural sector received around Rs. 5.00 for agricultural goods worth $1.00, but it paid over Rs. 8.00 for manufactured goods worth $1.00. Even if the estimates understated agriculture's rate and overstated that for manufacturing (though the estimating procedure would tend to produce the opposite bias), there is reason to suppose that agriculture gets about one-third less than it might under 'free trade'. Second, there has been a considerable narrowing of the gap between the implicit exchange rates for the two sectors since the mid-1950s, which is consistent with the hypothesis that the growth process worked off the disequilibrium of Partition and the trade policies adopted in the early 1950's. To take one of the most extreme points, around 1954/55 and shortly after the trade crisis, the figures suggest that agriculture received about Rs. 3.25 per dollar but paid around Rs. 9.50 per dollar, for the products it sold and bought. Again, even allowing for considerable bias in the projections of implicit exchange rates, agriculture in the mid-1950s must have received only 50 per cent of the value its sales would have bought if they could have been traded internationally without the limitations imposed by government policy. Third, even though a considerable portion of the disequilibrium between sectors was eliminated by 1959, there was still some narrowing of the gap after 1959. One could say that the process has been a continuing one for about a decade. Fourth, East Pakistan's farmers had worse terms of trade than did West Pakistan's in the 1950s, due both to a lower implicit rate for agricultural goods in East Pakistan and to a higher implicit rate for manufactured goods in that province.[1]

[1] Interestingly, however, the implicit rate for manufactured goods in East Pakistan was slightly lower than that in West Pakistan during the Second Plan period, for the weights used here. This result is due in part to the lower level of prices for imported goods in East Pakistan as reported by Pal, 'Domestic Prices of Imports: Extension of Empirical Findings', *Pakistan Development Review*, Winter 1965. In addition, price comparisons for such items as tea, paper, soap, matches, and cotton textiles in recent years show prices in East Pakistan are slightly lower than in the West wing.

The relation between the official exchange rate, with or without bonus for exports, and the implicit exchange rate for manufactured goods bears some mention. If the prices of imports and import-competing goods were related to the prices at official exchange rates, the implicit rate for manufactures would have risen, as did the official rate. Instead, of course, the implicit rate fell as the official rate rose. Indeed, in years following the devaluation in 1955, the implicit exchange rate for import-competing goods moved in the opposite direction from the price of foreign currency.

The terms of trade seen from the manufacturing sector's point of view are shown in Figure 9. The generally lower level of implicit exchange rates for East Pakistan manufacturing is due to the heavy weight of jute textiles in that province. Aside from that fact, the differential between the implicit exchange rates for goods the manufacturing sector produced relative to goods it bought are much narrower than in the case of the agricultural sector. The manufacturing sector received about Rs. 7.00 for manufactured goods worth $1.00, while it had to pay around Rs. 5.25 for agricultural goods of $1.00 in value in the mid-1960s. If some error is allowed in each exchange rate, the difference could not be more than about 20 per cent. In the mid-1950s, however, the manufacturing sector paid Rs. 3.50 for its agricultural purchases worth $1.00, and received more than Rs. 7.00 for sales worth $1.00. Again allowing for some error, the manufacturing sector must still have received about 75 per cent more for its output than it paid for purchases of equivalent value in world trade in the mid-1950s. The gap between the exchange rates for the two sectors was narrowed over the entire period after 1954/55, though rising agricultural exchange rates are responsible for more of the narrowing through 1959, while falling manufacturing exchange rates are responsible for the narrowing after 1959.

The differentials in the implicit exchange rates, or the differentials in world and domestic terms of trade of the two sectors, are less when viewed from the manufacturing sector's point of view than from that of agriculture. There are good reasons for this fact. First, domestic indirect taxes bring the implicit rate for manufactured goods facing producers below the implicit rate facing the agricultural sector. Second, the weighting schemes are very different in the two measures. The agricultural goods most discriminated against are jute and cotton, both of which have fairly high weights in marketings of the agricultural sector, but much of the output is exported, which reduces their weight in purchases by the manufacturing sector. Third, the investment and related goods industries have had rising implicit exchange rates in the latter part of the period, and since their weight is larger in production by manufacturing than in purchases by agriculture, the behaviour of the two weighted exchange rates is different. When viewed from either sector's point of view, however, the differences between the implicit exchange rates for agricultural and for manufactured goods was substantial in the mid 1950s, and while the gap narrowed considerably, it was still present in the 1960s.

These figures give some more quantitative information on the effects of Partition and the trade-restricting policies adopted thereafter on the profitability for domestic manufacturing industry. Obviously, those industries using domestically produced agricultural products as raw materials were given a tremendous boost by the fact that they could purchase inputs at a very low exchange rate and sell them at a high rate. Other things being equal, one would expect that manufacturing processes which were heavy users of agricultural raw materials would benefit greatly relative to those producers who used manufactured inputs. Since consumer goods industries (textiles, food products, tobacco) and two of the large intermediate (jute manufacturing and leather processing) were the principal users of agricultural raw materials, one would expect that they would be most profitable, and therefore have the greatest incentive to expand domestic production first.

It is clear from the movements of the implicit exchange rates over time that the economic costs of the trade-restricting policies were also being reduced. In terms of the analysis in Chapter II, the manufacturing industries moved quickly into the phase of falling domestic (relative to world) prices. There are other important aspects of this movement in manufacturing's implicit exchange rate. First, a part of the decline in domestic, relative to world, prices must have been not a reduction in costs, but a reduction of windfall profits going to those who were able to obtain the first licences to import textile machinery and other capital goods and sell output in the highly restricted domestic market. Second, the decline in industrial prices must represent some decrease in the real costs of production, if only because the index of relative prices of the major inputs into manufacturing, namely agricultural goods, was rising over the same period that the prices of manufacturing output were falling. Unfortunately, it is impossible to give an indication of the relative importance of these two explanations for the declining implicit exchange rate for manufacturing.

The Effects of Tax and Non-Tax Policy on Relative Prices and Incentives

The information on implicit exchange rates gives an opportunity to evaluate the relative effects of tax and non-tax policy on manufacturing prices through time. The detail and accuracy that was possible for imported goods reported in the last chapter cannot be achieved, but some more general conclusions are possible. Table 20 gives comparisons for the 3 years (1954/55, 1959/50, and 1963/64) for which tariff and domestic tax rate data were computed for the same industries. From the tax data and the official exchange rate, one can calculate an implicit exchange rate for each industry that would exist if domestic prices just equalled c.i.f. prices plus tariffs. The rates for each commodity on which I have also estimated implicit exchange rates over time were weighted and averaged in the same manner as were the implicit rates for each year. Table 20 gives the picture from the agricultural sector's point of view. If farmers had been forced to pay only the tariff-protected prices of goods in 1954/55, they could have purchased $1.00 of manufactures for Rs. 5.50 while it appears that actually they were forced to pay around Rs. 9.00 for these goods. The extent to which tariffs understated the 'true' exchange rate for manufactures fell by 1959/60 and by 1963/64, and weighted average tariff on manufactured goods that farmers purchased (Rs. 10.00) exceeded the implicit exchange rate for those goods (Rs. 8.00).[1]

[1] This is contrary to the evidence on imported goods only. The reason is that for several important industries, particularly textiles, domestic prices had fallen enough that the implicit exchange rate was below that implied by the tariff. That is, the industry was entering the 'falling domestic costs' phase (Phase III of the model in Chapter II) of its development, where tariffs were becoming redundant.

The implicit exchange rate for manufactured goods was falling, even though both the tariffs and the official price of foreign exchange rose over the period 1954–64. The same phenomenon appears from the viewpoint of the manufacturing sector, though there is less narrowing from 1954/55 to 1959/60 in the case of producer's prices.

TABLE 20. *Implicit Exchange Rates for Manufacturing from Price Comparisons Compared with Rates Implied by Tariffs and Taxes*

	Implied by Tariffs			*Implicit Rate Estimates*		
	1954/55	*1959/60*	*1963/64*	*1954/55*	*1959/60*	*1963/64*
West Pakistan						
Gross output weights, producer prices	4·95	6·64	8·90	7·45	8·36	7·57
Agricultural sector purchases of manufactures, market prices	5·37	7·63	9·98	8·59	8·97	8·25
East Pakistan						
Gross output weights, proproducer prices	4·72	6·70	7·69	6·57	7·51	6·55
Agricultural sector purchases of manufactures, market prices	5·28	7·58	10·10	9·63	8·94	7·73

Source: Exchange rates implied by tariffs were computed by multiplying each industry group by its average tariff from Chapter VI and weighting the exchange rates for industry groups by the weights given in Lewis and Hussain, *op. cit.* User's prices were those implied by tariffs (t_i) and producer prices were adjusted downwards for domestic indirect taxes ($t_i - t_{di}$). Estimated implicit exchange rates are from Lewis, *op. cit.*

Broadly speaking, tariffs understated the amount of protection that the manufacturing sector received during the early part of industrialization, but by the Second Plan period the weighted tariff had become redundant, and actual protection was lower than tariff-implied protection. The most recent movement was due both to falling implicit exchange rates for the goods and to rising tariffs on the same goods, but even in the First Plan period the gap between tariffs and implicit exchange rates had narrowed from its earlier position.

In order to evaluate better the movements in tariffs relative to those of implicit exchange rates, the manufacturing sector was divided into three groups used earlier: industries producing primarily (i) consumption goods, (ii) intermediate goods, and (iii) investment and related goods. The data on implicit exchange rates as estimated from price data are compared with the exchange rates implied by

TABLE 21. *Implicit Exchange Rates and Tariff-Implied Exchange Rates for Major Subsectors of Manufacturing*

	Rates Implied by Tariffs			*Implicit Exchange Rates*		
	1954/55	*1959/60*	*1963/64*	*1954/55*	*1959/60*	*1963/64*
East Pakistan						
Purchased by agriculture						
Consumption goods	5·35	7·71	10·48	9·81	8·95	7·60
Intermediate goods	4·90	6·75	7·38	8·48	9·32	8·41
Investment and related goods	3·94	6·21	6·33	6·98	8·46	9·18
West Pakistan						
Purchased by agriculture						
Consumption goods	5·47	7·90	10·63	8·45	8·84	7·78
Intermediate goods	4·80	6·20	6·77	8·68	8·31	9·67
Investment and related goods	3·94	6·41	6·54	8·61	9·86	9·31

Source: Same method as followed in Table 20. Tariff rates from Chapter VI, Implicit Exchange Rates from Lewis, *op. cit.*

tariffs in Table 21. The results are quite consistent with the findings in earlier chapters. Consumption goods industries had experienced a fall in prices relative to intermediate and investment goods, as reported in Chapter III, and by 1963/64 the tariffs on the consumption goods included here were on the average redundant. For intermediate and for investment and related goods, where imports are still an important share of total supply, quantitative restrictions on imports offset tariffs, and the estimated implicit exchange rates are above the exchange rates implied by tariffs. The reason that the implicit rate is below the tariff-implied rate for all manufacturing is the heavy weight of consumer goods industries in total manufacturing production and in the domestic use of manufactures.[1]

The results strongly support the view that non-tax and non-tariff policies have been more important than tariff and tax policies in setting relative prices over time. Such a conclusion is complementary to the results of analysing import prices only: quantitative restrictions, rather than costs or tariffs, set prices of imports. The present conclusion is even stronger. In a previously open economy, where trade is restricted and an overvalued currency is maintained, long-run cost considerations or indirect tax and tariff policy may have little or nothing to do with the whole structure of relative prices whether of imported or of domestically produced goods. Such a conclusion was suggested by Radhu with much more scattered evidence related to price changes and indirect tax changes.[2] Radhu found no evidence that increased indirect taxes had resulted in higher prices on the average. All this evidence is consistent with the view that the cost–price disequilibrium is manufacturing products was being worked off even into the 1960s. On the average, the disequilibrium has worked itself off farther in consumption goods than in intermediate and investment goods industries, though there are notable exceptions to any such general statement.[3]

The data in Table 21 support the view that, despite the differentiation in the tariff structure that favoured the domestic production of consumer goods, the effect of the licensing system outweighed it. In 1954–55, while averages of nominal tariffs for the industries covered

[1] The implicit rate on imported consumer goods was well above the tariff-implied rate, as noted earlier. The reason for the implicit rate for consumer goods as a whole to lie below the tariff-implied rate is the overwhelming importance of domestically produced consumer goods, many of which had lower implicit exchange rates, in the total supply of consumer goods. The heavy weight of cotton textiles was of particular importance.

[2] Radhu, 'The Relation of Indirect Tax Changes to Price Changes', *Pakistan Development Review*, Spring 1965.

[3] For example, jute textiles, paints and varnishes, sewing machines, fans, and some other electrical equipment are all exported from industries other than those producing consumer goods, indicating that they have met domestic demand and have exportable surpluses at competitive prices (when Bonus Vouchers are taken into account). Sugar and artificial silk textiles are notable exceptions to the general phenomenon of falling implicit exchange rates for consumption goods.

in Table 21 were 80, 50, and 30 per cent on industries producing consumption, intermediate, and investment and related goods, respectively, import licensing restrictions made domestic prices 194, 185, and 167 per cent above c.i.f. prices for the three groups of industries.[1] If these latter figures are of the right order of magnitude, the evidence supports the view that differential tariff protection was to a large extent offset by the general scarcity of all types of manufactures after the trade crisis. The implication of such evidence is that there must be reasons other than differential protection for the early development of the industries producing primarily consumer goods.

2. DIRECT IMPACT OF THE IMPORT LICENSING SYSTEM

In addition to the effects on relative price structure, the import licensing system had two other effects on the domestic allocation of resources. First, and closely related to the price problem, the licensing system created additional protection for those activities for which competing imports were licensed with unusual stringency. Second, since the system made some licences directly available to industrial users, it provided additional differentials in profitability: industrial licensees were able to obtain foreign exchange for raw materials both on a regular basis and at a price substantially below the level paid by non-licensed industrialists. Since the import licensing data that have recently become available include information on both the type of commodity that was importable under the licence and the type of industry to which industrial licences are granted, one may look at both sides of the effect of licensing patterns.

The quantitative information in this section is taken from the compilation and analysis done by Naqvi[2] on the basis of the licensing data supplied by the Chief Controller of Imports and Exports to the Pakistan Institute of Development Economics.[3] The data are

[1] West and East Pakistan rates were weighted 2 : 1 in this calculation to correct for the dominance of West Pakistan in both the absorption and the production of manufactured goods.

[2] S. N. H. Naqvi, *Commercial Policy and Resource Allocation.* Unpublished Ph.D. dissertation, Princeton, 1966.

[3] S. N. H. Naqvi, A. M. N. Chowdhury, and P. S. Thomas, *Basic Statistical Tables: Import Licensing in Pakistan, 1953–1964*, Research Report No. 35, P.I.D.E., Karachi, 1965.

not cross-classified by type of commodity and type of licence in all time periods, so completeness is not possible. They do give a firm indication of the direction in which the licensing system, by itself, was nudging (and reflecting) policy decisions about resource allocation.[1] The one major gap in the information is the lack of data on imports of machinery and equipment, which was not available with the data on other private imports.[2]

Naqvi's analysis of licences issued for particular types of goods (whether by industrial or commercial licences) during the 1950s yields the conclusions one would expect given the type of policy statements cited in Chapter IV. There was a decline in the share and sometimes in the level, of licences issued for consumer goods, and a rise in the share of licences issued for the import of raw materials (particularly raw materials for capital goods) and capital goods themselves.[3] Within the licences issued by type of good imported, the largest shift came in the reduction of the licences issued to commercial licensees for the imports of consumer goods. To the extent that the licensing decisions independently affected resource allocation decisions and the relative stringencies with which commodity imports were to be restricted, there was a tendency for the composition of imports to shift away from consumer goods towards raw materials and the products of the metal-working industries. In part, however, this shift reflected the policy of limiting more sharply the import of those things for which substitutes were already being produced at home. Since consumer goods industries, particularly those dependent on domestically available raw materials, were the first to develop

[1] One must add 'reflecting' resource allocation decisions since industrial licensing decisions were based on former permissions to import capital equipment to start an industrial undertaking.

[2] This problem is explained in P. S. Thomas, 'Import Licensing and Import Liberalization in Pakistan', *Pakistan Development Review*, Winter, 1966, and S. N. H. Naqvi, 'The Allocative Biases of Pakistan's Commercial Policy: 1953–1963', *Pakistan Development Review*, Winter 1966.

[3] The modified ECAFE classification of goods that Naqvi followed includes in 'capital goods' many items that might more easily be classified as intermediate products originating in the metal-working industries. The capital goods licences do not include the licences issued to industrialists for the purpose of importing equipment to set up a manufacturing plant.

productive capacity, imports competing with these industries were limited most sharply.

If the estimates of implicit exchange rates given in the last section are of the right order of magnitude for the early years, then the licensing system was almost as stringent with imports that competed with capital goods and intermediate manufacturing industries as it was with consumer goods, since the implicit exchange rates for those former industries were almost as high as the rates for the latter. Thus, Naqvi's finding that the pattern of import licences issued moved in the direction of limiting the imports of consumer goods relatively more than the imports of intermediate products, is consistent with either of two views: (i) the relative stringency of licensing determined the pattern of investment; or (ii) the pattern of investment and import substitution fed back into the decisions of the licensing authorities about relative desirabilities of permitting different types of imports. Given the statements by the Economic Appraisal Committee and others about the necessity for restricting imports more tightly *as soon as domestic substitutes became available*, the latter explanation seems more likely.

The second set of data brought out by Naqvi's analysis gives the pattern of industrial licensing between 1957 and 1963 by type of industry to which import licences were issued. The principal change in composition is a fall in the share of consumer goods industries and a rise in the share of the investment and related goods industries. Intermediate goods industries fell in relative importance until 1960, but rose sharply by 1963. Table 22 gives the data for the major groups of industries for 4 years, and it also contains the direct import coefficients for the same groups of industries for 1963/64. It is clear from the direct import coefficients that the consumer goods industries are the least import intensive, and the investment and related goods industries most intensive in import use. This is the counterpart of the overwhelming importance of domestic raw materials in the consumer goods industries which were set up first.

The rising share of the investment and related goods industries in total licences issued to industrialists reflects primarily the differential growth rates of the consumer goods and investment goods industries. The new capacity in investment and related goods industries must have received government sanctions since without such sanctions no import licences would be issued for raw materials. By 1963, one can see that the value of gross output of investment and

TABLE 22. *Value of Import Licences Issued to Industries Classified by Use of Products (Rs. million)*

	1957	*1959*	*1960*	*1963*	*Direct Import Coefficients 1963/64*
Industries producing primarily:					
Consumption goods	166·6	150·7	217·2	282·8	10·95
Intermediate goods	75·9	82·7	169·1	231·7	12·98
Investment and related goods	32·2	135·9	169·1	255·7	22·98
TOTAL	274·6	369·3	475·9	770·2	

Note: Totals may not add due to rounding.
Source: Naqvi, *Commercial Policy, op. cit.*, Appendix Table III. Import Coefficients are simple averages of industries taken from Chapter VI of this study, and are based on the Tims–Stern input–output table for 1963/64, which appears as an appendix in Planning Commission, International Economics Section, *Methodology for Estimating Import Requirements*, mimeographed, Karachi, 1965.

TABLE 23. *Annual Rate of Increase in Value of Import Licences Issued to Industries (percentages)*

			Annual rate of Growth of Gross Output	
	1957–60	*1959–63*	*1954/55–1959/60*	*1959/60–1963/64*
Industries producing primarily:				
Consumption goods	6·9	17·0	16·1	12·8
Intermediate goods	4·3	29	34	12·8
Investment and related goods	50	17·1	25	23
TOTAL	14·7	20	19·3	14·5

Source: Growth of industrial output from Chapter III, growth of imports computed from Appendix III of Naqvi, *Commercial Policy . . ., op. cit.*

related goods that had legitimate claim (in the government's eyes) to raw material imports must have been just under half of the value of consumption goods,[1] since the import coefficient of the latter is less than half of the former.

The differential growth rates in output of the various industries are not completely reflected in the growth of imported raw materials. This is due both to (i) a changing composition of output within industries, resulting in changing import coefficients, and (ii) differential growth rates of imported inputs between industries having different growth rates of output. The annual rates of increase of import licences and of gross output of the three types of industries are given in Table 23. Here, two main things are evident. First, during the late 1950s when foreign exchange was exceedingly scarce, even the rapidly growing industries producing consumer and intermediate goods must have been lowering their import components, or, alternatively, the industries with low import components were growing most rapidly. The converse was true of the investment and related goods industries, where the licences for imports of raw materials were growing even more rapidly than the exceedingly fast rate of growth of gross output. This may have been due to the rise of the metal-working industries sanctioned by the government in the late 1950s. Such industries used much greater proportions of direct imports in gross output than most other industries. In the 1960's the picture changes somewhat, with licensed imports growing faster than production for consumption and intermediate producers, implying rising import coefficients or the more rapid growth of import-dependent industries. The growth rate of output for the investment and related goods industries was somewhat slower than the increase in licensed imports.

Given the year-to-year variations in the licensing patterns, one can say only that despite the deceleration in the growth rates of gross output in the consumer and intermediate goods producing industries, the rate of growth of direct imports increased in the Second, as opposed to the First, Plan period. The particularly sharp change in the intermediate goods industries, which is reflected in most individual industries shown in Chapter VI, is due to an increase in investment in import-replacing (but import intensive) intermediate

[1] By 1963, however, the jute and cotton textile industries were meeting a substantial portion of their imported raw material and spare parts needs from Bonus Vouchers earned through exports.

goods at the end of the First, and the start of the Second, Plans. The average import coefficient for the several intermediate goods-producing industries has risen as new and modern plants have been established. Finally, it should be remembered that the increase in import licences issued is related to the 'import liberalization' program that began in 1959 with the beginning of greater inflows of foreign resources. Without the greater foreign exchange availability the pattern surely would have been much different.

The information on licences issued, combined with the price information of the preceding section, suggests that the licensing system was largely a mirror of the decisions to invest in different industries. First, the price data suggest that in the 1950s there were not large and systematic differences in nominal protection (including the effects of quantitative restrictions) given to industries producing different types of goods. Second, while the data on licences issued for competing imports are consistent with the fact that consumer goods industries developed first, they are also consistent with the view that licensing stringency on particular goods increased only *after* the domestic production of similar goods began. Third, the rapid increases in licences issued to industries producing intermediate and capital goods reflects prior decisions of private firms to invest in such industries and decisions by the government to sanction such investments. Thus, the licensing system and the overvaluation of the currency acted primarily to raise the profitability of manufacturing investment in general and did not have substantial effects favouring the consumer goods industries that have sometimes been alleged. The pattern of investment decisions must have been influenced significantly by other non-policy factors as well.[1]

3. OTHER INFLUENCES ON INVESTMENT DECISIONS

I have repeatedly emphasized the importance of the domestic production of raw materials by the agricultural sector as the principal basis for determining the industries that were first established on a

[1] For the argument that improper incentives misguided the economy in the 1950s see J. H. Power, 'Industrialization in Pakistan: A Case of Frustrated Take-off?', *Pakistan Development Review*, Summer 1963.

large scale in Pakistan. The evidence on implicit exchange rates for major groups of industries around the mid-1950s suggests that there was little in the prices of output relative to world prices that would have led to a choice of consumer-oriented goods by entrepreneurs making investment decisions. There are two other aspects of the problem. First, what were the sizes of the markets for output of the different types of industries? Second, what could be said about

TABLE 24. *Total Supply (at Market Price) of Products Classified by Industry According to Major Use (Rs. million)*

	1951/52	*1954/55*	*1959/60*	*1963/64*
Industry producing primarily:				
Consumption goods	1,953	1,856	3,270	5,448
Intermediate goods	332	656	1,649	2,711
Investment and related goods	449	795	1,934	4,592
TOTAL, all industries	2,734	3,306	6,853	12,751
PERCENTAGE DISTRIBUTION				
Consumption goods	71·4	56·1	47·7	42·7
Intermediate goods	12·1	19·8	24·1	21·3
Investment and related goods	16·4	24·1	28·2	36·0

Source: 1951/52 from Appendix: 1954/55, 1959/60, 1963/64 from S. R. Lewis and R. Soligo, 'Growth and Structural Change in Pakistan's Manufacturing Industry, 1954–1964', *Pakistan Development Review*, Spring, 1965. *Note:* the data for 1951/52 cover only eleven, instead of twenty-six, manufacturing industries, but there are some omissions from each of the three sub-groups of industries, and all omissions are relatively minor items, so the distribution should not be greatly affected.

the prices of inputs into the industries? Presumably, investment would be relatively more likely in those industries with large markets, particularly large domestic markets. Investment would also be more likely in the cases where the spread between input and output prices was relatively large.

While market size relative to efficient plant size would be the most appropriate measure of the first aspect of potential profitability, such information is exceedingly hard to come by. Table 24 gives the value of total supply (or total demand) of the three major groups of manufactured goods for the 4 years for which such data are available. It is clear that the market for consumer goods was much larger than either the market for intermediate or investment and related goods, or both combined, in the 1950s, and it was only in the last part of the First Plan and the early years of the Second Plan that the market for intermediate and investment and related goods became larger than that for consumer goods. This change in relative market sizes must have been closely related to the acceleration in investment activity in the same periods.

The other principal aspect of profitability is the spread between output prices and input prices. For industries based on raw materials produced by the agricultural sector the spread was large, with $1 worth of manufactured output worth Rs. 7.00 to Rs. 8.00 in the mid-1950s, and $1 worth of agricultural goods purchased worth Rs. 3.00 to Rs. 4.00. For industries based on intermediate products that had been processed by the manufacturing sector (either domestic or imported) the cost of $1 worth of intermediate manufactures *if purchased on the domestic market* was something over Rs. 8.00, approximately the same as, or slightly more than, the value placed by the domestic market on $1 worth of output of intermediate or investment and related goods. Such a consideration would be less relevant, however, if producers were able to meet all raw material needs through direct import. If import privileges were available they would have had to pay under Rs. 5.00 per dollar of intermediate goods. The figures in Table 25, however, give some notion of the relative amounts of (i) goods imported directly by industrialists and (ii) those that were resold by commercial importers (for which the price was the domestic market price, not the c.i.f. price plus duties). In 1954/55, the first year for which data are available, raw materials and 'capital goods' imported under commercial licences were over 45 per cent of the total supply of privately licensed imports of such goods, and even in 1963 the share of commercially licensed imports was about one-third of the total.

A substantial proportion of demand for intermediate goods was met from goods that were legally resold on domestic markets, and for which the domestic price was much higher than the c.i.f. price plus duties. This means, then, that there was another disincentive to the investment in industries producing any goods which depended on manufactured intermediate products. In the late 1950s, as suggested in the last section, the rate of investment in sanctioned capacity for producing intermediate and investment and related goods increased, increasing the claims of such producers on relatively cheap foreign exchange. But in the earlier period, any lag in the rate of investment and import substitution in the intermediate and investment goods industries must have been due not to the failure of

TABLE 25. *Comparison of Import Licences Issued for Raw Materials and Capital Goods on Industrial and Commercial Licences (Rs. million)*

	1954/55		*1957*		*1959*		*1963*
Raw materials and capital goods	302·7	(100·0)	366·7	(100·0)	405·9	(100·0)	n.a.
Commercial licence	153·4	(50·7)	148·2	(40·4)	159·2	(39·2)	382·7
Industrial licence	149·3	(49·3)	218·4	(59·6)	246·6	(60·8)	n.a.
Total value of industrial licences issued	185·6		274·6		369·3		770·2
Commercial licences for raw materials and capital goods as percentage of those licences *plus* total industrial licences	45·3		35·1		30·1		33·2

Note: Licences for fuels and lubricants were removed from the value of licences issued as appear in Naqvi's tables. The size of this item (over Rs. 235 million in 1954/55, 1957, and 1963) would distort the analysis, and they are not importable on industrial licence but are only imported with licences issued through the Oil Companies Advisory Committee (OCAC).

Source: Naqvi, Appendix Table 11.

quantitative controls to provide high domestic prices of output, but instead to the relatively smaller domestic markets for such goods and the higher relative prices of the manufactured inputs into their production.

4. POLICY AND NON-POLICY INFLUENCES AND THE STRUCTURE OF INDUSTRIAL GROWTH

A few remarks are offered here to bring together the material on the actual structure of growth and the various forces influencing the structure that evolved.

First, import substitution progressed earliest and most rapidly in the industries producing primarily consumption goods. A more important characteristic of the industries that first produced domestically, however, was their dependence on domestically produced, primarily agricultural, raw materials; and such intermediate goods industries as jute and leather processing certainly fall into this category. Second, the evidence presented in Chapter III suggests that there was an abnormally low amount of manufacturing activity in Pakistan at the time of Partition, and even if policy had tried to stay neutral with respect to relative prices of agricultural and manufactured goods, one would have expected the rate of growth of manufacturing output to exceed a 'normal' growth rate for a country of Pakistan's size and income level. Third, the size of the domestic market at Partition and well into the 1950s was decidedly larger for consumer goods than for most intermediate and investment and related goods. The differential market size was related to both the lack of manufacturing capacity in general (and hence a relatively low demand for manufactured intermediate products) and a low ratio of investment to income, with correspondingly low demand for capital goods. I think it fair to say that even if trade policy had tried to be neutral, the growth of total manufacturing would have been higher than 'normal', and import substitution would have occurred first and most strongly in the consumer goods industries.

Policy was not neutral, however. The most interesting question is the direction in which it was non-neutral, both consciously and unconsciously.

First, the government in the early years did not specifically opt for import substitution heavily in consumer goods industries to the exclusion of other goods. The intent of major recommending bodies was clearly not to so bias the choices. Heavy chemicals, fertilizers and light and medium engineering industries, all favoured by the Economic Appraisal Committee, are decidedly not consumer goods industries. The tariff structure that had emerged by the eve of the First Plan was not so greatly differentiated with the exception that basic metals and machinery production was not encouraged by the tariff structure alone. The sharp differentials and cascading of the tariff structure, particularly the changes that raised tariff rates on consumer goods and particularly textiles, did not come until the

1960s, after the scope for further import substitution in consumer goods was practically exhausted.

Second, the general approach to foreign exchange controls greatly biased the incentives to invest in different types of industries. The failure to devalue after the Korean War boom collapsed, in combination with export taxes on raw jute and cotton, kept agricultural prices very low, while the adoption of quantitative controls on imports raised the prices of manufactures much higher than those implied by tariffs. This by itself greatly encouraged those industries based on domestic agricultural raw materials.

Third, however, the nature of the administrative controls on imports made the domestic prices of imported intermediate goods much higher than the price implied by tariffs alone unless one had received government sanctions and had access to direct licensing and imports of raw materials. In the late 1950s and early 1960s permissions for establishment of domestic capacity in intermediate and capital goods industries did provide access to less expensive foreign exchange for industrialists receiving sanctions, and the extent of discrimination in favour of industries using domestic raw materials decreased somewhat.

It is clear that tariffs and indirect taxes played relatively minor roles in directing resource allocation, even when compared with other policy variables. Direct quantitative controls were dominant in setting prices and incentives. Through their substantial impact on relative prices, these controls speeded the process of structural change both by imposing the inducements to invest in various industries and by transferring substantial amounts of income to industrialists who reinvested them in the profitable manufacturing sector. The *directions* that industrial growth took were probably the same as those that would have been taken in the absence of major policy decisions due to market size and domestic resource availabilities. The policies adopted increased the *speed* with which the transformation of industrial structure occurred, both by increasing incentives and by increasing incomes in the hands of the 'saving' sector of the economy. Finally, while there have been substantial reductions in implicit exchange rates for manufactures, and while it appears that cost reductions must have taken place in parts of manufacturing, there remains a very large degree of distortion in the domestic price system relative to international prices, or trade opportunity costs, of the same goods. In addition, the 'liberalization' program of the mid-1960s tended to widen, rather than narrow, the deviations of domestic from world prices: the partial and selective removal of the quantitative controls on some imports, particularly on those with already relatively low duties, pushed the relative price structure farther away from world prices. The 'levelling' of incentives by general scarcity that existed in the mid-1950s was being replaced by a highly differentiated set of incentives for import substitution which will be further discussed below.

CHAPTER VI

A More Disaggregated view of Industrial Growth in Pakistan

The past three chapters have dealt with a very aggregative view of the industrialization process and of the measurable variables related to both policy and flows of goods in Pakistan. Most of the data in those chapters were built up from the more detailed estimates for individual industries. This chapter is concerned with those individual industry data. For the decade 1954–64, twenty-five to twenty-seven manufacturing industries could be distinguished, while for the early 1950s it was possible to reconstruct information on eleven important industries. The format followed in examining the growth process and structure is the same as that of the preceding chapters. First, the facts (or artifacts) are given about the growth that emerged and the relative price changes related to it. Then, the policy variables that could be measured, including information on tariffs, import licences, and the price effects of import controls, along with the comparisons with 'typical' patterns of growth, are examined in relation to the observed structure of industrialization.

1. RATES OF GROWTH AND TRADE RATIOS[1]

The growth rates of manufacturing industries separately and by groups of industries classified by major use of the output are given in Table 26, for the three time periods on which data were available. The data show higher rates of growth for total value added in manufacturing than are found in the National Accounts or in other estimates of value added in large-scale manufacturing, but a substantial part of the difference is due to the omission here of four slowly

[1] Parts of this section are based on my article with R. Soligo, 'Growth and Structural Change in Pakistan's Manufacturing Industry', *Pakistan Development Review*, Spring 1965.

TABLE 26. *Rates of Growth of Large-scale Manufacturing Industries in Pakistan, 1951–64*

	Gross Value of Output			*Gross Value Added*		
	1951/52– 1954/55	*1954/55– 1959/60*	*1959/60– 1963/64*	*1951/52– 1954/55*	*1954/55 – 1959/60*	*1959/60– 1963/64*
Consumer Goods						
Sugar manufacturing	4·4	14·3	21	7·2	13·8	15·8
Edible oils	28	18·1	28	28	19·1	23
Tea manufacturing	43	2·3	8·4	42	27	13·5
Food manufacturing N.E.C.	n.a.	27		n.a.	20·0	7·2
Beverages	n.a.	0·6	16·5	n.a.	0·6	7·0
Tobacco manufacturing	19·8	18·2	24	19·8	17·5	33
Cotton and other texiles	50	17·7	8·2	55	15·2	8·2
Silks and artificial silk textiles	n.a.	17·8	7·0	n.a.	16·1	8·2
Footwear	n.a.	12·2	4·9	n.a.	9·9	5·9
Wood and furniture manufacturing	n.a.	32	11·0	n.a.	41	17·4
Printing and publishing	n.a.	11·3	17·1	n.a.	12·2	17·1
Soaps, cosmetics, etc.	n.a.	31	6·4	n.a.	31	4·7
Matches		7·3	5·3		8·4	4·5
Miscellaneous manufacturing industries	n.a.	18·7	32	n.a.	19·8	32

Intermediate Goods						
Jute textiles		34	8·8		35	6·0
Paper manufacturing	n.a.	22	18·8	n.a.	22	19·9
Leather manufacturing	n.a.	35	3·8	n.a.	23	10·5
Rubber and rubber products	22	13·6	13·0	24	18·3	14·2
Fertilizer	n.a.	45	45	n.a.	50	55
Chemicals and pharmaceuticals	n.a.	30	18·2	n.a.	34	18·8
Petroleum and coal products	25	10·1	30	25	10·9	19·9
Investment and Related Goods						
Non-metallic mineral products	8·3	19·8	15·5	9·7	23	18·2
Basic metals	n.a.	14·8	43	n.a.	23	46
Metal products	n.a.	23	18·2	n.a.	27	25
(Basic metals and metal products)	23	19·2	30	28	25	38
Machines except electric	n.a.	33	24	n.a.	34	26
Electrical machinery and equipment	n.a.	40	29	n.a.	40	10·3
Transport equipment	n.a.	45	15·2			
Total Manufacturing	33	19·3	14·5	38	19·5	15·7
Consumption goods	39	16·1	12·8	43	15·6	12·8
Intermediate goods	23	39	12·8	28	27	13·7
Investment and related goods	17·2	25	23	16·8	28	26

Source: Computed from Appendix Tables and from Lewis and Soligo, *op. cit.*

TABLE 27. *Statistics on Production and Trade of Manufactures in Pakistan, 1951–64*

	Percentage of Production in Total Supply				*Percentage of Production Exported*			
	1951/52	*1954/55*	*1959/60*	*1963/64*	*1951/52*	*1954/55*	*1959/60*	*1963/64*
Consumer Goods								
Sugar manufacturing	22·8	49·7	99·9	99·5	0	0	2·1	2·3
Edible oils	63·6	95·4	96·6	78·3	0	0	0	2·8
Tea manufacturing	92·3	97·7	99·4	98·7	64·4	29·5	22·8	0
Food manufacturing, N.E.C.	n.a.	72·5	73·0	61·1	n.a.	1·8	12·9	18·1
Beverages	n.a.	71·2	62·2	66·0	n.a.	0	0	0·3
Tobacco manufacturing	88·6	98·5	99·6	99·7	n.a.	0	0.1	0·7
Cotton and other textiles	14·5	80·1	97·3	96·8	1·4	0·8	19·2	11·2
Silk and artificial silk textiles	n.a.	43·0	51·0	45·2	n.a.	0	0	0·2
Footwear	n.a.	99·8	99·8	99·2	n.a.	n.a.	n.a.	21·7
Wood and furniture manufacturing	n.a.	34·5	82·7	45·5	n.a.	7·5	1·9	2·1
Printing and publishing	n.a.	91·0	88·9	90·3	n.a.	0·6	1·7	0·5
Soap, cosmetics, etc.	n.a.	84·2	94·2	87·9	n.a.	0·1	0·8	11·2
Matches	10·9	97·0	100·0	100·0	0	0	0	0
Miscellaneous manufacturing industries	n.a.	34·2	37·4	57·4	n.a.	29·3	66·6	47·4

Intermediate Goods										
Jute textiles	5·3		99·4	99·9	100·0	16·3		56·2	79·9	86·4
Paper manufacturing	n.a.		49·4	66·6	72·1	n.a.		0·1	1·1	5·7
Leather manufacturing	n.a.		98·9	98·9	92·5	n.a.		86·6	98·2	77·4
Rubber products	25·4		40·9	33·9	30·7	0		0·1	1·3	10·8
Fertilizer	n.a.		20·0	41·9	75·6	n.a.		(187·2)*	54·7*	56·0*
Chemicals	n.a.		29·3	39·3	39·4	n.a.		10·3	9·8	9·6
Petroleum products	31·5		34·9	32·8	59·7	n.a.		10·4	10·8	1·6
Investment and Related Goods										
Non-metallic mineral products	80·0		80·6	78·0	65·9	0		0·7	0·6	1·9
Basic metals and metal products	14·2		44·0	44·0	44·0	0		1·7	5·4	1·8
Machinery	n.a.		6·4	12·7	15·4	n.a.		7·1	1·6	5·1
Electric machinery and equipment	n.a.		20·3	30·3	35·1	n.a.		1·2	0·1	3·7
Transport equipment	n.a.		14·0	34·5	24·3	n.a.		6·4	10·0	8·6
Consumer goods	22·5[a]	80·0[a]	76·9	91·7	88·7	7·6[a]	3·9[a]	3·8	13·2	8·2
Intermediate goods	26·8	49·3	47·6	59·1	65·0	0·5	26·4	32·4	51·7	39·9
Investment and related goods	23·7	51·0	28·2	35·3	34·6	0·0	2·7	2·2	3·3	3·3

* These coefficients are very high due largely to re-export in early years and exports to alleviate over-stocking in both early and recent years. Fertilizer is not yet an 'export industry' in the usual sense of that word.

[a] The totals refer to only the eleven industries for which we have all the data for 1951/52.

Source: Computed from Appendix Tables and from Lewis and Soligo, *op. cit.*

growing agricultural processing industries: grain milling, rice husking, cotton ginning and jute pressing.[1] One major characteristic of the growth rates in Table 26, as already noted, is the declining growth *rate* in total value added over each of the three successive periods. The deceleration is found in most individual industries and industry groups as well.

Even with the deceleration in growth rates, these manufacturing industries, which cover what can reasonably be called modern manufacturing, have been growing at rates of 15–20 per cent per year in current prices, and only somewhat lower in constant prices.[2] Domestic demand for manufactures was not rising so rapidly throughout the period, and some growth of output was going to exports, some replacing imports. Table 27 presents data on the same industries showing the share of domestic production in total supply and the proportion of domestic production exported for the 4 years under study. On import replacement, the pattern is quite clear. From 1951 to 1960, the share of domestic production in total supply of all three groups of industries increased consistently, with only five of twenty-six separate industries showing any decline. Total demand clearly rose less rapidly than domestic production over that period. During the Second Plan period, however, when the growth of GNP, investment, and imports accelerated sharply, demand for output of consumer goods and investment goods industries rose more rapidly than domestic supply. Apparently domestic demand was rising much more rapidly than export demand, since the ratio of exports to production fell in both the consumer goods and the intermediate goods categories.

In terms of the simple model outlined in Chapter II, most of the consumer goods industries were in Phase IIB of output growth (replacing imports at high cost) in the period 1954–59, and some apparently passed on to Phase III (falling domestic costs) and even Phase IV (competitive production for export) by 1960–64. Cotton textiles is the principal example of the latter movement, though shoes, soaps and cosmetics, and matches made a similar movement. Most of the investment goods industries and some of the intermediate

[1] The Appendix gives more complete details on the data problem.

[2] The price index for manufactures was rising only about 1 per cent per year from 1954 to 1964.

goods industries (e.g. rubber goods and chemicals) still provided less than half of total supplies from domestic production. On the other hand, except for miscellaneous manufactures (including primarily sports goods) and fertilizer (explainable by inventory problems) the only industries that were truly 'export oriented' were the jute textile and leather processing industries, both based on traditional primary export products. Several industries, however, had broken into export markets for 10 per cent or more of domestic production, an encouraging sign that domestic costs must have fallen to some extent. A marked contrast to the 'success' in most industries was the dismal failure of the tea industry, where domestic consumption rose much more rapidly than output, resulting in a complete elimination of tea exports by 1963/64. Broadly speaking, not only did imports decline in relative importance to domestic manufacturing in most sectors (including producers' goods industries) but also several industries broke into exports to a greater or lesser extent.

The extremely rapid rates of growth for total manufacturing and for major categories of industries are largely explainable first by the changing trade position in various industries, and in recent years by the acceleration in investment activity and related domestic demand. In the period 1954/55–1959/60 imports were more tightly restricted and large inflows of foreign assistance had not yet become available. In those years, there was a fairly clear relationship between the growth rates of gross output of industries and the trade-relatedness of their 'sources' of growth. For seven industries with more than 60 per cent of growth 'due to' import substitution or export expansion, the simple average of their growth rates was 39 per cent, six industries with 20–60 per cent of their growth 'due to' import substitution or exports had an average growth rate of 25 per cent; and twelve industries with less than 20 per cent of growth due to trade-related demand had an average growth rate of 13 per cent. High growth rate industries did have trade-related growth, while those that depended on domestic market expansion had lower rates of growth.

The Second Plan period in the early 1960s had a different pattern of growth. Import substitution and export growth 'contributed' very little to over-all growth of manufacturing industry, largely because of the acceleration in domestic demand, and in imports connected with the rise in investment rates and in aid-financed imports. Even so, the industries that did experience some import substitution during the period showed, on the average, markedly higher growth rates of value added than the average of industries not growing in response to import substitution. Eleven industries had import substitution make some contribution to growth, and they had a simple average annual growth rate of value added of over 23 per cent, while the average for all industries was under 16 per cent. Four industries besides those with import substitution as a source of growth had growth rates higher than the average, and two of those (non-metallic mineral products and basic metals and metal products) were closely linked with the acceleration in investment demand during the Second Plan.

Finding that trade-related (import substituting or export expanding) industries were growing faster than the rest of the industrial sector, however, does not tell us a great deal about whether rapid growth was related to any economic policy or to other factors.

2. RELATIVE PRICE CHANGES WITHIN MANUFACTURING INDUSTRY[1]

If the manufactures in which import substitution takes place do follow a series of Phases as outlined in Chapter II, one would expect to find reductions in the relative prices of those goods so long as: (i) the import substitution process gets past the stage of high-cost domestic production, and (ii) domestic demand is not increasing relative to domestic supply, since in such a case excess profits are made and the industry is not in long-run equilibrium.

In order to examine the changes in the relative prices within the manufacturing sector over the period under study, time trends were fitted to the individual price series in each industry. Differences in the trend coefficients indicate different rates of change of absolute prices and, therefore, changes in the relative prices among industries. We measured the relative price changes (or fit the trend lines) from the year at which the industrial sector had the best terms of trade of the

[1] The results in this section are drawn from my monograph with S. Mushtaq Hussain, *Relative Price Changes and Industrialization in Pakistan 1951–1964*, Karachi, 1967.

period (or the year when the agricultural sector had the worst). The coefficients thus derived tell something about the rate at which different industries worked off the disequilibrium in the market for manufactured goods in general by the restriction of trade.[1]

The rates of increase in absolute prices for manufacturing industries are given in Table 28. In West Pakistan, major consumption goods such as edible oils, cotton textiles, cigarettes, soap and matches, show either no significant trend or a slightly negative trend after 1954/55. These are goods in which import substitution through Phase II (limited, high-cost domestic production) was completed early, almost by 1954/55. The failure of these prices to rise, or the fact that some fell, in the face of a rising general price level suggests that these goods moved into Phase III of the model (falling domestic costs) over the period under study. Indeed, cotton textiles and soap were exported by 1959/60 and 1963/64, respectively, indicating they had moved into Phase IV (fully competitive domestic production), though at an exchange rate more favourable than the official rate. The same goods in East Pakistan show sharply negative trends for the most part. In both provinces, refined sugar, silk and artificial silk textiles, and tea, all consumption goods with high income elasticities of demand, showed rising trends in their prices. Demand in urban areas, particularly, was rising more rapidly than production. Shoes and footwear also had a rising price trend, even though there were exports from the industry in 1963/64. The rising trend in footwear prices is related to the rise in leather prices. Leather became an export industry quite early, and its prices are closely linked to the exchange rate for exports. Both shoes and leather were placed on the Export Bonus list in 1959.

Intermediate and investment goods industries show mixed results, though most prices were rising. Domestic demand was accelerating sharply over the entire period, putting strong pressure on prices. Metal products provides an interesting case, since its trend value of prices is not significantly different from zero, while prices in general were rising. Metal products and basic metal industries were not

[1] Two considerations of practical importance entered into the choice. One was the fact that more industries had price data by 1954 than in an earlier period. The second was that the analysis of industrial growth had its base year in 1954/55 for the largest number of commodities.

TABLE 28. *Annual Percentage Increase in Prices of Manufactured Goods, West and East Pakistan, 1954/55–1963/64.*

	West Pakistan	East Pakistan
Consumption Goods		
2070 Sugar manufacturing	4·6	5·0
2091 Edible oils	−0·79*	−3·9
2092 Tea manufacturing	3·2	2·4*
2099 Food manufacturing N.E.C.	3·9	−2·0*
2100 Beverages	1·8	−0·06*
2200 Tobacco manufacturing	0·18*	−2·2
2311, 2390, 2490 Cotton and other textiles	1·2	−0·76
2314 Silk and artificial silk textiles	7·9	7·9
2420 Footwear	3·7	2·2
2500, 2600 Wood and furniture manufacturing	1·8	−0·06*
2800 Printing and publishing	1·8	−0·06*
3150 Soap, perfume, etc.	0·91*	−1·6
3193 Matches	−0·72	−2·4
3900 Miscellaneous manufacturing industries	1·8	−0·06*
Intermediate Goods		
2313 Jute textiles	—	3·1
2700 Paper manufacturing	3·5	2·9
2900 Leather manufacturing	5·6	3·8
3000 Rubber and rubber goods	1·3	2·0
3114 Fertilizer	—†	—
3199 Chemicals and pharmaceuticals		
Chemicals	4·6	−0·17*
Pharmaceuticals	—	0·12*
3200 Petroleum and coal products	2·3	2·0
Investment and Related Goods		
3300 Non-metallic minerals	2·8	—
3400 Basic metals	4·2	6·7
3500 Metal products	0·93*	0·98*
3600 Machinery except electrical	1·3*	6·7
3700 Electrical machinery	—	—
3800 Transport equipment	—	—

* Not significant at the 95 per cent level of confidence.
† Blank indicates no observation for 1954/55.
Source: Lewis and Hussain, *op. cit.*

separated in the analysis of growth, due to problems with import tax data classifications. The two industries are quite different, however. The rates of import tax on basic metals and on metal products in 1963/64 were 17 and 66 per cent, respectively. A substantial portion of metal products output in Pakistan is light hardware and kitchen utensils. Working with imports c.i.f. and output at factor cost, which overstates the relative contribution of domestic production, the ratio of domestic output to total supply in metal products was 85·2 per cent in 1954/55, 78·5 per cent in 1959/60 and 68·9 per cent in 1963/64. If one assumes that the increased imported share after 1954/55 represented primarily non-consumer goods, then it would appear likely that Phases IIB and III (output growth and falling domestic costs) were the appropriate stages of the consumer goods portion of the metal products industry after 1954/55. Indeed, kitchen utensils were exported to some extent by 1963/64. Metal products industries may be another industry that has passed through all early phases and is entering Phase IV of fully competitive domestic production (at a more realistic exchange rate) for a substantial part of its output.

There are some interesting differences between East and West Pakistan in the relative price coefficients in consumer good industries. In most cases the price of consumer goods fell significantly in East relative to West Pakistan. Since prices for domestically produced and imported goods were quite close in the two provinces in 1963/64, the result implies that consumption goods prices in East Pakistan were significantly higher than those in West Pakistan in the 1950s. This finding is consistent with the earlier results reported on the terms of trade, and the implication that East Pakistan's farmers had become a greater burden than farmers in the West following the restriction of trade in the early 1950s.

3. NON-POLICY DETERMINANTS OF GROWTH IN INDIVIDUAL INDUSTRIES

Before looking at the policy-related variables, one can examine other aspects of the industries that experienced import substitution earliest or most rapidly. Using the same procedure and data as given in Chapter III, the 'normal' or 'typical' pattern of the ratio of domestic production to total supply in various manufacturing industries was calculated from Chenery's studies.[1] The results are given in Table 29 for a country of $75 *per capita* income and 100 million population. It should be recalled that these would be extreme values of both

TABLE 29. *Proportion of Domestic Production in Total Supply of Manufactures*

	'Typical' Country	*Pakistan 1951/52*	*1954/55*	*1959/60*	*1963/64*
2000/2100/2200 Food, beverages and tobacco	0·962	0·415	0·778	0·944	0·885
2300 Textiles	0·868	0·129	0·786	0·944	0·934
2400 Footwear and clothing	0·977	n.a.	0·998	0·998	0·992
2500/2600 Wood and furniture manufacturing	0·938	n.a.	0·345	0·827	0·455
2700 Paper manufacturing	0·629	n.a.	0·494	0·666	0·721
2800 Printing and publishing	0·977	n.a.	0·910	0·889	0·903
2900 Leather manufacturing	0·933	n.a.	0·989	0·989	0·925
3000 Rubber manufacturing	0·852	0·254	0·409	0·339	0·307
3100/3200 Chemicals/petroleums, coal products	0·842	n.a.	0·176	0·564	0·568
3300 Non-metallic minerals	0·958	0·800	0·806	0·780	0·659
3400/3500 Basic metals and metal products	0·913	0·142	0·440	0·440	0·440
3600/3700 Machinery including electrical	0·169	n.a.	0·092	0·180	0·222
3800 Transport equipment	0·413	n.a.	0·140	0·345	0·243

Source: 'Typical country' is computed from Chenery, 'Patterns of Industrial Growth', *American Economic Review*, September, 1960, for imports, and United Nations, 'A Study of Industrial Growth'. New York, 1963, for production computed for a country of $75.00 *per capita* income and 100 million population. Pakistan data are from Appendix Tables.

independent variables in the Chenery study, since countries of $300 *per capita* and 10 million in population are more 'typical'. The comparison is of interest, however, since the Pakistan coefficients, in

[1] H. B. Chenery, 'Patterns of Industrial Growth', *American Economic Review*, September 1960. United Nations. *A Study of Industrial Growth*, New York, 1963.

the early years especially, are very different from the 'typical' pattern.

To the extent that the 'typical' pattern represents true comparative advantage as measured by the two independent variables (which it cannot do precisely since countries did not follow neutral policies),[1] the built-in characteristics of the economy would lead it to return to or to move towards the 'normal' pattern if it were driven away from it by either exogenous or policy-related shocks. Partition, of course, was such a shock. Much of the import substitution that occurred in Pakistan could be interpreted, according to Table 29, as a movement back towards a 'normal' pattern of industrial structure in response to changed profitabilities of investment, and not directly related to policy changes or directions. The movement towards 'normal' patterns would be a reason for the import substitution in the food, beverages, and tobacco industries, textiles, paper, machinery and equipment, and some of the growth of the transport equipment and rubber products industries. Using the figures for 1959/60 (the year at the end of the more 'restrictive' 1950s, marking the first break into the exports of manufactures in any significant amount) there are four industries with greater than 'expected' proportions of domestic production in total supply: textiles, footwear, leather products, and paper and paper products. As shown below, these industries were relatively highly protected by tariffs throughout the period; but they were also export industries by 1960, in the sense that they were exporting a significant share of their output. Rubber products, chemicals and petroleum products, basic metals and metal products, and transport equipment are all industries with less than 'predicted' shares of domestic production in total supply, but machinery and equipment industries had a higher share of domestic production in total supply than the 'typical' pattern suggested.

A comparison of Pakistan's structure of production with the Indian structure in the same post-Partition period is quite suggestive of the types of industries that Pakistan might have developed had she been a separate country before 1947. The data for India are again taken from the study by J. Ahmad. Ten industries are compared for the very early 1950s, and seventeen for the mid-1950s in Table 30.

[1] See Chapter III for a discussion of the normative significance of the coefficients computed from the Chenery cross-section data.

TABLE 30. *Percentage of Domestic Production in Total Supply of Manufactured Goods: India and Pakistan Compared*

	Pakistan 1951/52	India 1950/51	Pakistan's Imports from India as percentage of imports from all sources 1954/55	Pakistan 1955/56	India 1949/50
Sugar refining	22·8	100	n.a.	49·7	100
Edible oils	63·6	98	38	95·4	96
Tea	92·3	100	100	97·7	100
Cotton and other textiles	14·5	98	13	80·1	97
Silk and artificial silk textiles	n.a.[a]	78	30	43·0	83
Footwear	n.a.	100	n.a.	99·8	100
Soaps, etc.	n.a.	100	100	84·2	100
Matches	10·9	100	n.a.	97·0	100
Jute textiles	5·3	100	100	99·4	100
Paper products	n.a.[a]	63	5	49·4	65
Rubber products	25·4	94	16	40·9	95
Fertilizers	n.a.[a]	20	n.a.	20·0	85
Petroleum products	31·5	46	n.a.	34·9	56
Chemicals and pharmaceuticals	n.a.[a]	74	17	29·3	83
Non-metallic mineral products	80·0	100	n.a.	80·6	100
Basic metals[b]	14·2	62	7[c]	44·0	60
Electrical machinery and equipment	n.a.	63	n.a.	20·0	64
For later years only	*1959/60*	*1960/61*			
Non-electrical machinery	12·7	42			
Transport machinery and equipment	34·5	61			

[a] No basis for estimating domestic output from modern industry. With the possible exception of pharmaceuticals, however, it was probably negligible, implying coefficients of close to zero for these industries in 1951/52.

[b] Indian data are for basic metals only. Pakistan data are for basic metals and metal products.

[c] Imports are not accurately broken down here, but for both Indian and non-Indian sources, the data include the machinery, millwork, hardware instruments and metals categories of goods.

Sources: Pakistan data from Table 27. Indian data from J. Ahmad, *Import Substitution and Structural Change in Indian Manufacturing Industries, 1950–1956*, Memorandum No. 17, Project for Quantitative Research in Economic Development, Harvard University, Cambridge, 1966. Data on imports are taken from Pakistan, Department of Commercial Intelligence, *Foreign Trade of Pakistan, July 1950–June 1951*, Karachi, 1952.

Striking differences in the share of production in total supply appear between India and Pakistan around 1951, particularly in sugar refining, cotton and jute textiles, matches, rubber products, and basic metals and metal products. For several other industries where production data are not available in Pakistan, one can assume that production is small.[1] If this is true, then the differences between Indian and Pakistani structure are even greater. In a number of industries, not only was Indian production large with respect to total supplies of goods in India, but India also exported some manufactures of these categories to Pakistan, as is shown in the centre column of Table 30. Indeed, India was a major supplier (even in 1949/50) of the edible oils, tea, cotton, jute, and artificial silk textiles, soaps, rubber products, and chemicals and pharmaceuticals imported into Pakistan. One should recall, too, that the raw materials for the cotton and jute textiles that India exported to Pakistan were in large part exported to India from Pakistan.

Most industries in Pakistan began with very low ratios of production to total supply, which was a concomitant of the very low manufacturing base at Partition. By 1954/55, however, some industries had expanded to the extent that they were supplying shares of the domestic market almost as large as similar industries in India. It is particularly instructive to examine the industries which quickly supplied large shares of the domestic market: edible oils, tea, cotton, textiles, footwear, soaps, matches, jute textiles and non-metallic mineral products.[2] These are the types of industries for which Chenery found relatively low elasticities of production with respect to market size, so that one would expect the share of domestic

[1] Such industries as soap manufacturing, leather tanning, footwear manufacture, production of artificial silk textiles, paper production, manufacture of chemicals and pharmaceuticals, and production of machinery and transport equipment are examples of industries where domestic production must have been very small. Physical production data were not kept on these industries until large units were established, which did not occur until the early to mid-1950s.

[2] Scattered information on imports and import taxes indicates that there were substantial imports in the early years of footwear, soaps, and leather. There are no production data for these industries. Imports of these goods had fallen off substantially by 1954/55, as domestic production replaced imports.

production to rise rapidly in Pakistan relative to India. In several other industries, namely rubber products, paper products, chemicals, basic metals, and the machinery and equipment industries, Pakistan did experience rising shares of domestic production in total supply, but they did not rise as high as the shares of comparable industries in India. To the extent that the countries were similarly endowed (though India does have greater mineral resources than does Pakistan) one would expect these two countries to develop similar types of industrial structure, with the exception of those industries dependent on large size of market. This is in fact the kind of development that occurred. Thus, a substantial part of the increased manufacturing output that occurred in Pakistan after Partition, particularly through the 1950s, must have been due to the readjustment of productive structure to changed cost and price structures domestically following the creation of a new and separate economic unit in 1947.[1]

The Influence of Domestic or Imported Raw Materials

The domestic availability of raw materials may well have influenced the process of import substitution. The industries above the 'typical' share of domestic production in the Chenery comparisons were principally those dependent on domestic agricultural raw materials, while those that had not import-substituted as much as would be 'typical' were by-and-large those dependent on imported raw materials. A similar phenomenon also appears in the comparison with the Indian data. Table 31 contains the direct import coefficients for the individual manufacturing industries in 1963/64.[2] These data

[1] One could object to India as a basis for comparison of shares of production in total supply of manufactures, since India followed an autarkic policy of industrial growth through the 1950s and 1960s. It is for this reason that the comparisons between India and Pakistan were limited to the earliest years for which comparable data could be obtained. In this way, one could hope to approximate the industrial structure that existed just prior to Partition. Note that for the industries compared here, India experienced relatively little increase in the share of production in total supply over the period 1950/51–1955/56.

[2] The data are computed from the 1963/64 input–output table for Pakistan produced by W. Tims and J. J. Stern, which appears as An Appendix to Pakistan Planning Commission, International Economics Section, *Methodology of Estimating Import Requirements*, mimeographed, Karachi, 1965.

TABLE 31. *Direct Import Coefficients for Twenty-six Manufacturing Industries*

Industries Producing Primarily:		*1963/64 Direct Import Coefficient*
Consumer Goods		
2070	Sugar manufacturing	0·48
2091	Edible oils	7·51
2092	Tea	0·62
2099	Food necessities	5·76
2100	Beverages	5·98
2200	Tobacco	12·88
2311, 2390, 2490	Cotton and other textiles	6·41
2314	Silk and artificial silk textiles	32·83
2420	Footwear	4·22
2500, 2600	Wood and furniture manufacturing	5·77
2800	Printing and publishing	15·65
3150	Soap and cosmetics	30·69
3191	Matches	1·55
3900	Miscellaneous manufacturing industries	23·25
Intermediate Goods		
2313	Jute textiles	4·02
2700	Paper and paper goods	11·52
2900	Leather	11·14
3000	Rubber and rubber products	21·77
3114	Fertilizer	2·17
3199	Chemicals and pharmaceuticals	16·32
3200	Petroleum and coal products	10·92
Investment and Related Goods		
3300	Non-metallic minerals	5·60
3400	Basic metals	38·30
3500	Metal products	25·52
3600	Machinery except electrical	20·90
3700	Electrical machinery and equipment	24·10
3800	Transport equipment (Basic metals and metal products combined)	31·94

Source: $\sum_j m_{ji}/X_i$, or direct import coefficient, is computed from the Tims–Stern input–output Table for 1963/64, *op. cit.*

are indicators of a number of characteristics of the industries. If one ranks industries by import coefficients, presumably the ones with lower import coefficients are more dependent on domestically produced raw materials and factors of production, though since Table 31 has only direct and not total coefficients this would not necessarily be true.[1] If imports are tightly controlled, as they were in Pakistan over the period of this study, then there is another, and policy-related, aspect to the direct import coefficient: industries with heavy 'requirements' for imported goods, or limited possibilities for substitution of domestic factors or raw materials for imported ones, will be at a disadvantage relative to those which have low dependence on imports, or greater possibilities for substitution.[2]

One striking characteristic of Table 31 is the prevalence of high import coefficients in the intermediate and the investment and related goods industries, and the relatively few consumption goods industries that have high import coefficients. In order to explore the relationship between the share of production in total supply and the import coefficient, regression equations were fitted to the direct import coefficient and the share of domestic product in both 1959/60 and 1963/64. The regression coefficient was significant at the 0·5 per cent level, and the direct import coefficient explained 30–35 per cent of the variance in the share of production in supply in both 1959/60 and 1963/64. The importance of imported inputs (or its inverse, the importance of domestic raw materials and factors) *was* significantly related to the pattern of production that had emerged by the end of the 1950s and into the mid-1960s. While only one-third of the differences among industries could be explained by the import

[1] Analysis of industries by import coefficients and the distinction between direct and total coefficients is discussed thoroughly in M. Bruno, *Interdependence, Resource Use and Structural Change in Israel*, Jerusalem, 1962.

[2] Remember that *after* investment had taken place, the producer was entitled to *some* quantity of cheap foreign exchange as an industrial licensee. In the early years, however, a substantial proportion of raw materials was resold. Most producers, therefore, faced higher raw material prices. The statement in the text assumes that most investment decisions are more likely to be made by producers thinking of domestic prices of imports, not c.i.f. prices.

coefficients, this is considerably more, as will be seen, than the tariff structure can explain.[1]

The results of the regression exercise and the analysis of 'typical' structures of production suggest that a principal determinant of the structure of production and import substitution that emerged in Pakistan was not related *directly* to economic policy, but was more closely related to other aspects of the cost structure of the economy. In particular, investment decisions were related to the availability of domestically produced raw materials as a basis for a large number of manufacturing industries. The pattern of investment and import substitution also may have been related to that more difficult to define phenomenon, comparative cost advantages that go with (i) market size (as influenced by population)[2] and (ii) the complex of

[1] A problem with all the explorations into 'explaining' the pattern of import substitution that occurred faces one here, and it should be discussed briefly in connection with the data on import coefficients. The procedure followed to explore the relationship between the import coefficient and the pattern of import substitution was to compare (in this case by simple regression analysis) the import coefficient with the share of domestic production in total supply at the end of some period, either 1959/60 or 1963/64. There are obvious problems with this method but there are more serious problems with some alternative solutions. If one used the *change* in the share of production in total supply as the dependent variable, then all those industries which had had import substitution before the initial period would not be statistically related to the independent variable, even though that independent variable might have been the principal reason for the earlier import substitution in that industry. If one could be sure that the share of production in total supply had not been influenced by any policy or non-policy variable in the period before the base from which one measured the change, then it might be appropriate to use the change in the share as the dependent variable. Much of the early phases of import substitution in Pakistan (high cost domestic production behind trade barriers) had occurred before 1954/55, when the first comprehensive data become available. The change in the share of domestic production from 1954/55 to 1959/60, therefore, does not give a good measure of, e.g., the effects of import restrictions on the growth and import substitution in the domestic industry. For this reason, I have taken as the dependent variable the share of domestic production in total supply of the good at the end of the period, recognizing that this is not the best variable.

[2] Market size is another variable not related to policy directly that would be interesting to explore. It is most difficult to do so, however, since presumably the important determinant of import substitution as it

relative costs and factor endowments associated with *per capita* income. The importance of these variables was suggested by comparison with Chenery's studies and by the comparisons with the Indian data.

4. INCENTIVES FROM THE TARIFF AND INDIRECT TAX SYSTEM

(written with Ghulam Mohammad Radhu)

It should be clear from Chapters IV and V that the tariff and tax system was not the only nor the primary determinant of the difference between world and domestic relative prices of goods. It is worth examining the tariff structure, however, since it is the only explicit statement one has of the distortions the government was trying to create in the price system, or the directions in which it was trying to push domestic profitability. Indirect taxes in Pakistan have consisted of four types of taxes, on three types of flows of goods.[1] Export taxes were levied on major primary exports, particularly cotton and jute.

[1] A detailed review of all the indirect taxes and how they work is given by G. M. Radhu, 'The Rate Structure of Indirect Taxes in Pakistan', *Pakistan Development Review*, Autumn 1964; and their revenue importance is discussed in S. R. Lewis and S. K. Qureshi, 'The Structure of Revenue from Indirect Taxes in Pakistan', *Pakistan Development Review*, Autumn 1964.

---

relates to market size is the size of the market relative to efficient plant size. A part of what Chenery measures in his 'normal' patterns of import substitution is no doubt related to the market size variable, so that in examining Pakistan's pattern relative to the 'normal' pattern market size had implicitly been considered once. Other than the obviously large market that existed domestically for cotton textiles, even in the early years, attempts to relate simply the total demand for the output of the industry with import substitution in the industry were not particularly successful. Markets of $50 to $100 million in metals and metal products and in machinery and equipment developed in Pakistan by the mid-1950s, but these did not show high shares of domestic production in total supply, while industries with relatively small domestic markets (and presumably small efficient plant sizes) such as footwear, printing and publishing, matches, and leather goods, had high shares of domestic production in total supply.

Import duties were levied on imports. Excise taxes were imposed on domestic production of certain goods, usually after domestic production was firmly established in some relatively homogeneous commodities (cotton cloth, jute textiles, petroleum products, cigarettes, etc.). Finally, sales taxes applied to both imports and domestic production, though this was sometimes done at different and sometimes at similar *ad valorem* rates. Also, goods that were exported were exempt from the domestic excise and sales taxes. For goods subject to the export tax, the domestic price is the f.o.b. price minus the export tax, and domestic users receive a subsidy relative to the f.o.b. price. For goods subject to a domestic excise or sales tax, the domestic price is the f.o.b. price plus the domestic tax, and the domestic user pays a tax relative to the f.o.b. price.[1]

The types of protection measured and discussed below are called (i) nominal tariffs (t_i), in which we have included sales taxes on imports; (ii) nominal protection to production ($t_i - t_{di}$), which is the nominal tariff minus the rate of domestic indirect tax on production; and (iii) implicit or effective protection (T_i or U_i, as defined in Chapter II), which is the protection to the manufacturing process, or to value added in the industry.

There are several points to raise about the use of effective rather than nominal protection. First, the main reason for using effective rates is to take account of (i) tariffs on inputs that either offset or accentuate the nominal protection and (ii) the fact that low nominal protection may still result in high effective protection in industries with extremely low value added ratios. Second, while there may be important welfare judgments connected with the measures of effective protection, such welfare judgments are *not* our interest in this section. We want merely a measure of the extent to which various industries were encouraged domestically, and the effective rate of protection is one possible measure of such encouragement. Third, the calculated rates of effective protection should not be discussed separately from the nominal rates on the same industries.

One interesting question is the extent to which the nominal structure differs from the effective structure. Such considerations are particularly true when a significant part of the tariff structure is

[1] Both these statements about taxes and subsidies relative to the f.o.b. price assume that the world demand for the good is elastic.

TABLE 32. *Percentage Rates of Nominal Tariff, Nominal Protection, and Effective Protection in Pakistan, 1954/55 and 1963/4*

	1954/55			1963/64		
	t_i	$t_i - t_{ai}$	U_i	t_i	$t_i - t_{ai}$	U_i
Consumption Goods						
Sugar manufacturing	63	58	170	62	55	109
Edible oils	46	40	106	44	42	100
Tea manufacturing	18	14	22	14	−2	−60
Food manufacturing N.E.C.	37	31	56	77	70	71
Beverages (non-alcoholic)	90	72	88	107	81	90
Tobacco manufacturing	131	98	94	185	110	106
Cotton and other textiles	70	58	97	153	133	147
Silk and artificial silk textiles	125	98	93	200	174	121
Footwear	46	43	47	91	76	76
Wood and furniture manufacturing	43	36	174	64	54	201
Printing and publishing	0	0	−17	0	0	−13
Soaps and cosmetics	49	36	−13	73	38	1
Matches	132	97	91	95	33	38
Miscellaneous manufacturing	65	55	53	72	57	54
Intermediate Goods						
Jute textiles	48	38	63	70	51	92
Paper and paper products	46	39	61	77	62	83
Leather goods	64	54	156	99	91	216
Rubber and rubber goods	51	40	72	41	25	39
Fertilizer	0	0	43	0	0	28
Chemicals and pharmaceuticals	34	28	57	33	24	28
Petroleum and coal products	40	25	46	57	−23	−55
Investment and Related Goods						
Non-metallic minerals	71	59	56	69	49	40
Basic metals	24	18	20	19	9	3
Metal products	48	41	83	66	59	247
Machinery except electrical	5	5	−5	12·5	12·5	14
Electrical machinery and equipment	39	28	28	45	32	33
Transport equipment	49	45	115	55	49	256
Industries Producing Primarily:						
Consumption goods	65	53	76	88	66	74
Intermediate goods	40	32	71	54	33	60
Investment and related goods	39	33	49	46	35	81[a]

Note: T is used wherever U_i is negative, as U_i degenerates for negative values.

[a] The rate for basic metals and metal products combined is used to eliminate some of the distorting effects of the rate on metal products alone.

Source: See Appendix for methods of calculations.

really just a correction for the overvaluation of the domestic currency, and when the tariff structure alone does not set the difference between world and domestic relative prices.

Comparisons of effective protection, nominal protection and nominal tariffs are given in Table 32 for 1954/55 and for 1963/64 for each of the industries whose growth was considered above. Averages for the industry groups are also given. Considering first the relations between nominal tariffs and nominal protection $(t_i - t_{di})$ one can see that the introduction of domestic indirect taxes markedly reduced the differential incentive to consumption goods industries. In 1954/55, for instance, three industries had nominal tariffs in excess of 100 per cent but had their nominal protection reduced to under 100 per cent by domestic taxes. Tariffs were raised so sharply after 1960, however, that three industries in 1963/64 had nominal protection of over 100 per cent. There are very few cases in which $(t_i - t_{di})$ gives a significantly different picture of the relative amount of protection than does (t_i), even though introduction of (t_{di}) does reduce the absolute *level* of protection.

The theory of implicit or effective protection suggests that different incentives were given to various manufacturing industries than would be inferred from the nominal tariff or the nominal rate of protection. The main expectation that one might have from the literature on effective protection would be that the effective rates would generally be above the nominal rates, in some cases would be much higher, and would generally change the ranking of industries by degree of protection as well. In Pakistan, rank correlation showed there was no significant difference between the ranking of industries by nominal or by effective protection. The main effect of differential tariffs on inputs and on outputs, then, was to exaggerate the degree of protection given to value added.

In 1954/55, the bulk of the industries in Pakistan had rates of nominal protection near the level of effective protection. Eight of the twenty-seven industries had effective rates (U_i) less than the nominal rate of protection $(t_i - t_{di})$. Of these eight, three industries (printing and publishing, soaps and cosmetics, and non-electrical machinery) had negative effective protection (i.e. the weighted tariffs on inputs more than offset the protection to output). The extreme observations in the other direction are of particular interest. The three widest extremes, leather and leather goods, sugar refining, and wood and furniture products all were industries with low ratios of value added to gross output, so that any nominal tariff would greatly raise potential rewards to domestic factors of production. In wood and furniture production a large proportion of non-traded inputs also contributes to a high effective rate. Edible oils production has a very low value added ratio, and tariff rates are cascaded, resulting in an unusually high rate of effective protection. Cotton textiles had a high effective rate of protection in part because of the subsidy implicit in the export duty on raw cotton. Metal products, rubber products, and transport equipment all have significant tariff cascading, which accounts for their high effective tariff.[1]

The deviations of effective from nominal protection are more marked in 1963/64, due primarily to the sharp changes in tariff structure in favour of differentially high tariffs on consumer goods after 1960. The industries that show much higher effective than nominal protection are approximately the same group as in 1954/55: leather and leather goods, metal products, wood and furniture, transport equipment, sugar, and edible oils, for the same reason mentioned above. Jute textiles show a larger difference between nominal and effective protection. Soaps still show lower effective than nominal protection, as do tea, and petroleum and coal products, all due to substantial domestic indirect taxes.[2] The simple averages of the rates of effective protection are not particularly meaningful. There are industries within each group that enjoyed very high rates

[1] Automobile manufacture is a favourite example of the students of effective protection, since it is an industry in which all parts can be imported at lower tariffs than the tariff on the final good, and with a relatively low value added ratio in the assembly process, the nominal rate of protection can greatly understate the effective rate of protection to the process. Such is the case in Pakistan in the transport equipment industry. For a detailed study of automobiles in Chile see L. L. Johnson, 'Problems of Import Substitution: the Chilean Automobile Industry', *Economic Development and Cultural Change*, January 1967.

[2] The rate for petroleum and coal products probably overstates the extent to which domestic production is 'penalized' by the tariff and tax system. Most of the rates are either specific or are a combination of *ad valorem* and specific, and there is substantial room for error in this industry. The domestic and import taxes are very high and do tend to offset each other, however.

of effective protection while others in all groups had low or negative effective protection.

The absolute level of protection, whether nominal or effective, that was provided to some manufacturing industries was very high indeed, whether one considers a period near the beginning of industrial growth or one more recent. The range of tariff protection was substantial as well, with some industries being discriminated against by the tariff and tax structure, while others were given protection that would enable domestic producers either to make extraordinary profits or to operate at normal profits with extraordinary waste in terms of their use of intermediate goods or domestic factors of production. There was a tendency for consumer goods production to be favoured and production of machinery discriminated against by the tariff structure, though there was a very substantial range of protection on industries producing all types of goods: consumer, intermediate, and investment goods. It was not until after at least a decade of rapid industrial growth (and, as has been seen above, substantial reductions in domestic costs) that the level of protection to some of the consumer goods industries was raised differentially. In both earlier and later years, nominal rates were fairly good guides to effective rates of tariff protection except for some industries in which value added ratios were low and tariff levels were sharply cascaded. Such industries, however, were not all in any particular sub-group of industries.

Now that we have some measures of the extent and the differentiation of the tariff protection to various industries in earlier and more recent periods (and recognizing that tariffs were probably overcome by other factors such as import licensing policy) we can examine the relationship between the tariff structure and the pattern of import substitution that appeared. Once again we use as a dependent variable the percentage of production in total supply in a recent period, not the change in the share of supply coming from domestic sources, for the reasons discussed above.

In order to examine rigorously the relationship between the policy variables and the share of production in supply for various industries, linear regression equations were fitted between the proportion of production in total supply (both in 1959/60 and in 1963/64) and the six measures of tariff protection given in Table 32. No form of the tariff variable was significant even at the 10 per cent level. The results for 1959/60, before the effects of the 'import liberalization' program, were marginally better than those for 1963/64 for the tariff variables, but they were still not statistically significant. Finally, in order to see if the imported inputs into an industry from the same industry of origin (e.g. steel ingots into steel re-rolling, both of which are in basic metal industries) had distorted the results, we subtracted such inputs from total supply and used this share of domestic production in adjusted total supply as the variable to be explained. Again, no tariff variable was significant even at the 10 per cent level, but the direct import coefficient was still a significant variable.[1]

Multiple regression analysis was used to test the joint effects of protection and import coefficients as determinants of the share of domestic production in total supply.[2] The performance of the nominal tariff and protection variables improved, particularly in explaining the structure in 1959/60, i.e. before the effects of the import liberalization program. (Effective, or implicit, protection is still unrelated to the share of production in total supply.)

The two variables combined explain 40–45 per cent of the variance in importance of domestic production, or the extent to which 'import substitution' had occurred at some time in the past. About one-third of the variation in the share of domestic production is related to import coefficients in the industry, and about 10 per cent is

[1] The relevant data for t-tests on the regression coefficient and the R^2 for the equations are:

Dependent Variable	X_i/Z_i *1963/64*		X_i/Z_i *1959/60*		$X_i/\hat{Z}_i$ *1963/64*	
Independent Variable	*t-statistic*	R^2	*t-statistic*	R^2	*t-statistic*	R^2
t_i 1954/55	1·00	0·040	1·32	0·068	1·20	0·056
$t_i - t_{ai}$ 1954/55	1·20	0·057	1·64	0·100	1·21	0·057
U_i 1954/55	0·50	0·010	1·50	0·086	1·33	0·069
$t_i - t_{ai}$ 1963/64	0·76	0·024	1·48	0·083	0·78	0·025
U_i 1963/64	0·33	0·005	0·86	0·030	0·37	0·006
$\sum_j m_{ji}/X_i$ 1963/64	3·65	0·357	3·29	0·310	3·49	0·337

$\hat{Z}_i$ is total supply minus deliveries of imports from industry j to industry i.

related to nominal protection. There is not much difference in the regression coefficients for the tariff variables, and practically none in the import coefficient variable, among the various regressions tried. A fairly typical result would be given by:

$$\frac{X_i}{Z_i}(1959/60) = 76\% + 0{\cdot}26(t_i\ 1954/55) - 1{\cdot}6\,\frac{\sum_j m_{ji}}{X_i}.$$

---

[2] Relevant data for t-tests on the partial regression coefficients and the R^2 for the regression equations are:

Dependent Variable	X_i/Z_i *1963/64*		$X_iZ/_i$ *1959/60*		$X_i/\hat{Z}_i$ *1963/64*	
Independent Variable	*t-statistic*	R_2	*t-statistic*	R_2	*t-statistic*	R_2
$t_i - t_{ai}$ 1954/55	1·491	0·413	1·980[c]	0·411	1·473	0·394
$\sum_j m_{ji}/X_i$	3·740[a]		3·480[a]		3·577[a]	
$t_i - t_{ai}$ 1963/64	1·407	0·408	2·279[b]	0·437	1·404	0·389
$\sum_j m_{ji}/X_i$	3·864[a]		3·809[a]		3·706[a]	
t_i 1954/55	1·564	0·419	1·905[c]	0·404	1·538	0·398
$\sum_j m_{ji}/X_i$	3·786[a]		3·497[a]		3·620[a]	
t_i 1963/64	2·069[c]	0·458	2·279[b]	0·437	2·027[c]	0·437
$\sum_j m_{ji}/X_i$	4·062[a]		3·653[a]		3·881[a]	
U_i 1954/55	0·501	0·364	0·779	0·328	0·440	0·342
$\sum_j m_{ji}/X_i$	3·566[a]		2·849[a]		3·398[a]	
U_i 1963/64	0·495	0·363	0·838	0·331	0·458	0·343
$\sum_j m_{ji}/X_i$	3·591[a]		3·263[a]		3·435[a]	

[a] Significant at 0·5 per cent level.
[b] Significant at 5 per cent level.
[c] Significant at 10·0 per cent level.

This equation says that an industry with zero tariff and import coefficient of zero would have had 76 per cent of total supply produced domestically in 1959/60. A 10 percentage point increase in the rate of tariff would add 2–3 per cent to the share of total supply produced domestically, while an increase in the import coefficient by 10 percentage points would lower the share of domestic production by 16 per cent. An increase in the import coefficient of 1 percentage point would require a tariff increase of over 5 percentage points to keep the industry at the same share of domestic production in total supply. The low share of production in total supply, or the failure of 'import substitution' to occur in many intermediate and capital goods industries is closely related to their heavy import dependence and only of secondary importance was the lower tariff protection they were given.

The reliance on imported versus domestically produced raw materials or factors of production is a much more significant variable than tariff protection in explaining the industrial structure that evolved in Pakistan. Such a result is hardly surprising, but it does suggest that a principal reason for the early growth and extensive 'import substitution' in industries producing primarily consumer goods is the relative availability of domestic inputs for such products. This is not to say that positive inducements and incentives were unimportant, but simply that it would have taken a peculiar set of incentives to induce development that was different in many significant aspects from the pattern that in fact emerged. A different system of allocating foreign exchange, at a price closer to an equilibrium exchange rate, combined with lower differential protection to domestic industries might have resulted in, e.g., less soap or artificial silk cloth production, since these are industries with high direct import coefficients. But soap is now exported in several forms, and the effective rate of tariff protection is extremely low, so it hardly qualifies as an over-protected, high-cost industry. With only three notable exceptions, jute textiles (an export-oriented industry), fertilizer (which is being developed rapidly) and non-metallic mineral products (chiefly cement, which is subject to internal disputes between public and private sector development), all other intermediate and investment goods industries have high import coefficients, and might well be at a cost disadvantage relative to most consumer goods industries even if the exchange rates were at an equilibrium level and the industries were without differential protection. This is even more true if economies of scale (or market size) were more important in these industries, as was mentioned above. Thus, starting with the direct import coefficients and the knowledge that foreign exchange was scarce and, therefore, valuable relative to domestic resources, one would predict an industrial structure closer to the one that evolved than one would by using nominal rates of protection. Effective rates of tariff protection are of no help at all as explanatory variables for the industrial structure that appeared.

5. QUANTITATIVE RESTRICTIONS AND TARIFFS AS DETERMINANTS OF RELATIVE PRICES IN INDIVIDUAL INDUSTRIES

It is quite clear from Chapters IV and V that the tariff and indirect tax system had little to do with setting relative prices domestically, and that the principal determinant of the differences between world and domestic prices were quantitative restrictions. Unfortunately, the data on international prices over time by individual commodity group are not particularly good, and while it seemed reasonable to look at these price indices when averaged over a number of commodities, it would more likely be misleading for any single commodity or commodity group. The data on implicit exchange rates for recent years[1] give a basis for examining the relations of tariff rates and actual price ratios at the end of the period about which we were concerned, and allow some further speculation about the effects of economic policy and economic growth in Pakistan over the entire period. A comparison between nominal tariffs and estimated actual price differentials for most of the industries with which this study has been concerned are given in Table 33. The industries can be divided into three major groups related to the model of the import substitution process in Chapter II.

[1] The implicit exchange rates are based on direct price comparisons made by M. L. Pal, 'The Determinants of the Domestic Prices of Imports', *Pakistan Development Review*, Winter 1964; 'Domestic Prices of Imports: An Extension of Empirical Findings', *Pakistan Development Review*, Winter 1965; and by S. R. Lewis and S. E. Guisinger, 'Measuring Protection in a Developing Economy: The Case of Pakistan', *Journal of Political Economy*, October 1968.

TABLE 33. *Rates of Nominal Tariff and Estimated Actual Price Differences between Domestic and 'World' Prices in Pakistan, 1963/64*

Industries Producing Primarily:	*Nominal Tariff*	*Percentage by Which Domestic Price Exceeds 'World' Price*
Consumption Goods		
Sugar refining	62	327
Edible oils	47	106
Tea manufacturing	14	39
Cotton textiles	159	56
Silk and artificial silk textiles	200	350
Footwear	91	66
Printing and publishing	0	28
Soaps	73	94
Matches	95	62
Miscellaneous manufacturing industries		
Plastic goods	107	236
Sports goods	72	60
Pens and pencils	61	155
Intermediate Goods		
Jute textiles	70	46
Paper products	77	94
Leather products (tanning)	61	56
Rubber products	41	153
Fertilizer	0	15
Chemicals	33	81
Petroleum products	57	107
Investment and Related Goods		
Non-metallic mineral products		
Cement	69	75
Other products	69	154
Basic metals	17	66
Metal products	66	95
Machinery and equipment		
Sewing machines	85	60
Others	12·5	89
Electrical machinery and equipment		
Electrical appliances	104	308
Other electrical equipment	22	60
Transport equipment		
Motor vehicles	93	249

Source: Lewis and Guisinger, *op. cit.*

First, there are those few industries that have passed through the early Phases of high-cost domestic production. These industries have had large enough increases of domestic supply (i) to allow prices to become less than those implied by tariffs, and (ii) in some cases to export. The most notable of these is the cotton textiles industry, but footwear, sports goods, jute textiles, leather products and sewing machines are industries which exported by the 1960s, and matches had prices less than those implied by tariffs but did not export. Soap is a curious case, since while the domestic price is above the one implied by the tariff rate, there are exports! This phenomenon is due to a high domestic excise tax from which exports are exempt. Finally, it should be recalled that the price differentials were measured at the official exchange rate, while the exports of most industries took place at a price of foreign exchange from 20 to 60 per cent higher than the official price, due to the effects of the Export Bonus scheme.

In the second group of industries, competing imports had been cut back sharply, but domestic production was still limited relative to domestic demand, and prices were greatly above those implied by tariffs. Sugar is a prime example of this, though edible oils, silk and artificial silk textiles, plastic goods, pens and pencils, petroleum products, paper and paper products are also in this general category. The main effect of domestic expansion in this group of industries would be the reduction of costs; more domestic production would not 'save' imports directly.

Finally, there were the industries in which import substitution was still in the early stages, where imports had been restricted and there was relatively limited, relatively high-cost domestic production. In these industries the determining factors in domestic prices of both imports and domestic production were the quantitative restrictions on competing imports, not tariff rates. These industries include primarily intermediate and investment and related goods industries, such as rubber products, chemicals, non-metallic mineral products, basic metals and most metal products,[1] electrical and non-electrical equipment and machinery, transport equipment, and also some consumer durables such as electrical appliances and automobiles.

[1] Some items of hardware and utensils, which developed in the 1950s, were exported by the 1960s.

In this group there is considerable room both for expanded domestic production to replace imports and for reductions in costs of domestic producers.

Without reliable time series data on international prices, one can only imply what the changes in implicit exchange rates have been in the various industries. It is clear from the data in Chapter V that the prices of virtually all manufactured goods in the mid-1950s were well in excess of the prices implied by tariffs. About the best one can say is that in 1963/64 the industries for which the implicit exchange rate was less than that implied by the tariff (particularly those that have become export industries) have had falling implicit exchange rates over the period and have passed through the major phases of the import substitution process. For another group of industries, those in which domestic production is much less than total supply, the interpretation of implicit exchange rates is also fairly clear: in those industries, even though the rate of expansion of output has been very high, the rate of growth of domestic demand has also been high, so that imports have not been replaced by domestic production; and because of import restrictions and the general scarcity of the goods, these industries have had implicit exchange rates that exceed, and in some cases greatly exceed, the prices implied by import taxes.

But what about the group of industries in which domestic production largely replaced imports, but in which the domestic prices are still very high relative even to those implied by tariffs? Why have not prices fallen in these industries? There are three explanations that seem to apply in Pakistan, though they do not exhaust the possibilities. First is a relatively simple case in which domestic demand has simply expanded faster than production capacity in the industry, thus keeping the price from falling. Sugar refining was one example of this in Pakistan, and tea also was an industry in which domestic demand exceeded the growth of output, resulting in rising domestic prices and a collapse of tea exports. The second explanation for high implicit exchange rates is related to monopoly or oligopoly power in the industry, supported by the general restriction on competing imports. Paper was a good example in Pakistan, since paper was produced cheaply enough to export, but domestic prices were above those implied by either tariffs or the exchange rate for exports. There were only single producers of the major kinds of paper, which made dual pricing on the part of manufacturers relatively easy to accomplish.

Finally, there is a mixed and exceedingly interesting case that applies to several industries. The economics of the situation is illustrated in Figure 10. The basic point is that there can be a further

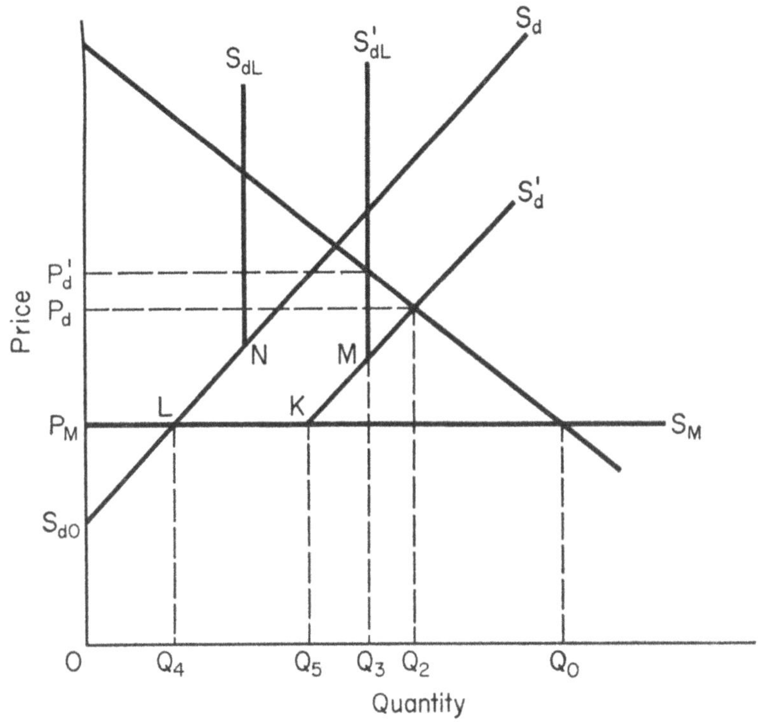

FIGURE 10. Effects of quantitative restrictions on imported inputs.

limitation on supply besides the restriction of imports of competing goods: if there is an input specific to an industry, there may be a supply limitation on domestic output related to the scarcity of raw materials. In the absence of any quantitative restrictions, if $S_{do}S_d$ is the supply curve for domestic production and P_mS_m is the imported supply curve, OQ_4 is produced domestically, Q_4Q_O is imported, and the price is P_m. If imports are restricted to Q_4Q_5, the supply curve for the good becomes $S_{do}LKS_d'$, OQ_4 plus Q_5Q_2 is produced domestically, and the price is P_d. Now, suppose that a major input, specific to the industry, is restricted in supply (also by quantitative controls on imports). The supply curve of domestic output would be changed to $S_{do}LNS_{dL}$. Allowing the Q_4Q_5 imports again, the supply curve of imports and domestic production of the good is $S_{do}LKMS_{dL}'$, and the domestic price is P_d', which is, of course, higher than P_d.

The sort of phenomenon described above seems to have been important in several industries in Pakistan. Plastic goods, where the raw plastic imports are limited, and silk and artificial silk textiles, where the yarn is imported but heavily restricted, are perhaps the best examples of this. Both have an additional symptom of this case, that they run at considerable excess capacity. The constraint on domestic production is not capacity, or monopoly restrictions, but input availability. Other items of the sort that could be classed as consumer luxuries also fall into a similar category, such as automobile assembly and assembly of transistor radios (in the heading of electrical appliances in Table 33).

It should be clear from the above discussion that, once again, quantitative controls, both on competing imports and on important raw materials, have been major sources of price distortion and differential incentives in Pakistan, and that they continue to be for large parts of the manufacturing sector. It is also clear, however, that a number of manufacturing industries have passed through the major Phases of the import substitution process. It should also be evident that there is a great variance in the stage of the import substitution process in which various industries found themselves in the mid-1960s, and that there was little systematic variation by type of good so far as the *price* variables were concerned. The major reason for the impression in Chapters III–V that the consumption goods industries were farther along in the process was that the cotton textile industry, which has by far the largest weight, had passed through all Phases and was successfully exporting by 1959/60. But there were industries in all major groups classified by product use that were exporting by the mid-1960s, and there were also industries in all major sub-groups that were at the limited high-cost domestic production stage of their development. Finally, since the industries were at such different stages of development by the late 1950s and early 1960s, and since it is impossible to reconstruct with any accuracy the protection received from all sources in the early 1950s, it was impossible to make any meaningful rigorous analysis such as that tried with tariff rates and import coefficients. The extent of disequilibrium in each of the variables was too great, and the attempt to identify the stage in which each industry found itself by the mid-1960s has been given as a substitute.

6. DIRECT IMPACT OF THE IMPORT LICENSING SYSTEM ON THE INDUSTRIAL STRUCTURE

One effect of the system of import licensing was on the relative price structure and the differential incentives to import substitution or industrial expansion. Naqvi's classification of data on import licences actually issued give an opportunity to look more closely at the direct impact of the licensing system in (i) restricting imports of the competing goods and (ii) providing imports of intermediate goods and spare parts to industrialists. One should remember that the receipt of licences to import directly was a substantial source of profit, due to the high scarcity value of such intermediate goods. Naqvi's data are not classified in precisely the same way as are the industrial output, trade, and tax data, but there is a great deal of similarity. It is possible to reconstruct for a list of industries comparable to that with which this chapter is concerned, the licences issued for imports competing with fourteen manufacturing industries, for almost a decade, and the licences issued to industrialists producing output of twenty-four different manufacturing industries corresponding roughly to those on which output data were available. Annual rates of increase in import licences issued for each type of good or for each industry are given for several periods of time in Table 34.

The evidence on licences issued for competing imports is quite scattered. Licences for tobacco products, cotton, silk, and artificial silk textiles, soaps and cosmetics were restricted progressively throughout the period 1953–63. While paper products is a mixed category in Naqvi's classification scheme, it, too, was being restricted insofar as one can tell. These are the industries in which import

TABLE 34. *Annual Percentage Rates of Increase in Import Licences Issued to Producing Industries and for Competing Imports*

Industries Producing Primarily:	*Licences Issued for Competing Imports* All Private Licences 1953/54–1958–59	*Licences Issued for Competing Imports* Commercial Licences 1959–63	*Licences Issued to Industry Competing with Imports* 1957–60	1959–63	1957–63
Consumption Goods					
Sugar refining	—	—	1·8	11·1	12·5
Edible oils	—	—	negative	44	14·8
Tea	—	—	negative	19·4	10·6
Food manufacturing N.E.C.	—	—	6·1	11·7	8·6
Beverages	8·5	4·1	negative	negative	negative
Tobacco	negative	negative	negative	15·5	−1·5
Cotton and other textiles			negative	9·4	−1·0
Silk and artificial silk textiles	negative	negative	41	17·1	−43·8
Footwear	—	—	77	42	41
Wood and furniture manufacturing	negative	—	40	11·9	9·0
Printing and publishing	—[a]	—[a]	negative	4·2	−1·0
Soaps and cosmetics	negative	negative	42	40	29
Matches	—	—	—	—	—
Miscellaneous manufacturing industries	—	—	—	—	—
Intermediate Goods					
Jute textiles	—	—	negative	negative	—8·4
Paper and products	negative[b]	6·8[b]	105	67	92
Leather products	—	—	negative	29	13·8
Rubber products	3·5	19·0	negative	23	14·8
Fertilizer	—	—	—	—	—
Chemicals and pharmaceuticals	negative	18·0	30	29	25
Petroleum and coal products	10·2	negative	77	7·0	43
Investment and Related Goods					
Non-metallic mineral products	14·9	negative	66	29	35
Basic metals	—	—	185	17·1	67
Metal products	—	—	104	4·1	39
(Basic metals and metal products)	31	43	138	11·0	51

Machinery except electrical	negative[c]	21	70	24	47
Electrical machinery and equipment	negative[c]	negative	50	40	48
Transport equipment	16·1	27	31	8·6	32

[a] The category 'Paper and products' includes printed matter in Naqvi's classification.

[b] One of Naqvi's categories that includes board and newsprint declined to zero in 1963, and dominates the decline from 1953/54 to 1958/59.

Source: Computed from Appendix Table in S. N. H. Naqvi, *Commercial Policy and Resource Allocation*, unpublished Ph.D. dissertation, Princeton, 1966.

substitution was progressing quite rapidly. There are other changes that are related systematically to the import substitution process. Competing imports of petroleum products expanded rapidly in the 1950s, but with the construction of a new refinery and rapid import substitution in the industry in the early 1960s, there was a decline in the growth of competing imports. The changes in machinery and in electrical machinery and equipment licences bear mentioning, since it is quite clear that imports of these goods were expanding rapidly, though these data do not so indicate. The problem is basically that the private sector imports of machinery to set up new capacity are not licensed through the regular procedure, and they do not appear in these data. However, it is of interest to see that the commercial imports of such goods were not expanding at a rapid rate, and to recall that these two industries were both experiencing import substitution throughout the period. Finally, competing imports of the rubber products industry were expanding very rapidly in the early 1960s, which was a time when the industry was having 'negative' import substitution.

If the above cases are typical, then it is fairly clear that the licensing system did behave in a manner consistent with the pattern of import substitution that occurred. If it is true that 'all' manufactures were scarce in the mid-1950s, however, then it is likely that the commercial import licensing policy followed other decisions: *after* domestic capacity had been established, competing imports were restricted relatively more by the licensing authorities. That is, differentially tight import licensing did not necessarily determine investment decisions but was a factor in protecting the domestic industry after that industry was established. This is consistent with the view

(i) that it was not necessarily the industries that were relatively more protected by licensing or by tariffs in which domestic capacity was established, and (ii) that other factors such as availability and price of raw materials, and domestic marketability of the output, led investors to choose among the variety of products that, in effect, were protected across the board by the general restrictions on imports.

The growth rates of import licences to industries producing particular goods are also given in Table 34. In general, the pattern of growth rates of import licences issued is related somewhat to the pattern of growth rates of manufacturing industries given earlier. With some exceptions, such as footwear, silk textiles, and a few other extremes, the rates of growth of industrial import licences issued correspond roughly to the rates of increase in output. Using the data on import coefficients in the various industries in combination with the data on licences actually issued (both of which are given in Table 35), one may examine more closely the relationships between the industrial licensing decisions and the rates of growth and levels of output of industries in the most recent period, 1959/60–1963/64.

The imports implied by multiplying (i) the import coefficients of the input–output table by (ii) the estimates of gross output in the various industries, correspond quite closely to the actual industrial import licences issued in 1959 and 1959/60.[1] There are only a few industries for that year for which the two magnitudes do not agree fairly well. Three of these (cotton, jute, and silk and artificial silk textiles) were all supplying some of their intermediate 'requirements' by importing under Bonus Vouchers, so that the industrial licences issued were not as great as the implied use of exports for this industry. Transport equipment has higher import licences issued than implied imports, for which I have no ready explanation. Finally, chemicals and pharmaceuticals and soaps

[1] In both cases licences issued in the calendar year (1959 and 1963) are related to the output figures and the implied imports of raw materials in the year lagged 6 months (1959/60 and 1963/64). The rationale for such a procedure is that the issuance of the licence is not simultaneous with the import of the goods, and certainly not with the use of the good in manufacturing production.

have deviations of licences from imports that almost exactly offset one another, so that if there were errors in either classification

TABLE 35. *Relation of Import Licences Issued to Imports Implied by Import Coefficients and Gross Output*

	Imports c.i.f. as percentage of Gross Output	*1959 Import Licences*	*1959/60 Implied Imports*	*1963 Import Licences*	*1963/64 Implied Imports*
Sugar	0·39	2·83	0·84	4·31	1·79
Edible oils	7·29	14·92	16·99	63·49	45·03
Tea	0·51	2·63	0·79	5·36	1·10
Food manufacturing N.E.C.	4·57	5·97	4·08	9·31	3·71
Beverages	4·79	0·49	1·03	—	1·90
Tobacco	4·06	10·27	8·89	18·25	20·72
Cotton textiles	5·60	56·77	90·75	81·37	124·58
Silk textiles	17·18	1·05	13·98	1·97	18·30
Footwear	3·33	3·29	2·47	13·41	2·99
Wood and furniture manufacturing	4·56	0·65	0·66	1·02	0·99
Printing paper products	11·64	7·79	7·38	9·20	13·87
Soaps	26·67	16·83	28·24	64·59	36·00
Matches	1·33	—	0·77	—	·95
Jute	3·50	0·26	13·16	0·24	18·70
Paper	9·43	4·78	8·14	37·01	16·21
Leather	9·19	5·85	15·07	16·04	17·52
Rubber	19·59	6·54	5·40	14·96	8·81
Fertilizer					
Chemicals and pharmaceuticals	11·52	30·61	18·46	85·58	41·14
Petroleum and coal products	8·43	9·76	13·53	12·73	39·15
Non-metallic mineral products	4·76	12·34	7·87	34·23	14·00
Basic metals	35·24	31·63	35·88	59·42	148·42
Metal products	24·21	32·87	37·12	38·66	72·31
Machinery except electrical	17·39	5·38	12·30	12·67	28·81
Electrical machinery and equipment	18·03	16·56	12·98	63·37	35·61
Transport equipment	18·06	52·62	21·70	71·16	38·09

Note: The import licences issued to various industries were for intermediate goods and spare parts used by the industry receiving the licence.

Source: Import coefficients (imports c.i.f. divided by output at market prices) computed from the Tims–Stern input–output table, *op. cit.* 'Implied imports' are the import coefficient times the gross output at market price for the appropriate year, from Lewis and Soligo, *op. cit.* Import licences issued are computed from Appendix Tables in Naqvi, *op. cit.*

system (for the input–output table or for licensing data), a combined chemicals and soaps industry would have almost the exact amount of implied imports as licences issued.

In 1963 and 1963/64, the pattern of implied imports is not so similar to the pattern of import licences issued. There is a close correspondence, however, between the industries deviating in Table 35 and those that have different growth rates of (i) import licences issued and (ii) output from 1959 to 1963. The changing characteristics and output mix of the industries explains the patterns of deviations. For example, there are nine industries for which the growth rate of import licences issued for raw materials greatly exceeded the growth rate of output from 1959 to 1963. In six of these (soaps, footwear, paper products, edible oils, non-metallic mineral products, and chemicals), the import licences issued were greater than the implied imports in 1963. If the import coefficients for these industries are correct, or nearly so, then the output of these industries in 1963/64 must have been greater than has been estimated. If the base period (1959/60) output is correct, the growth rate should be higher. On the other hand, the import coefficient may be incorrect, and the industries may have become more import-intensive over the period of the early 1960s. This was certainly the case with the edible oil industry, where domestic supplies of vegetable oils proved to be inadequate, and imports of raw materials have been growing relative to output. Paper is another industry that has made a special plea, based partly on arguments about greater quality output (and, therefore, inputs) needed for exports, to have a greater share of its raw material needs come from foreign sources, thus raising its import-intensity.

The other major group of industries is that for which the growth of output in the early 1960s was greater than the growth of import licences issued for raw material imports. Three of these industries also had implied imports greater than import licences issued in 1963 (basic metals, metal products, and petroleum products). The two metal industries can be explained in large part by the import 'liberalization' program that made imports of iron and steel items more readily available through commercial import licences, so that all 'requirements' for raw materials did not have to be met from industrial import licences.

The basic kinds of information that emerge from the data on

import licences that Naqvi has compiled serve primarily to reinforce the conclusions that have been reached in earlier sections. It is, unfortunately, impossible to say how much the licensing system influenced the pattern of import substitution and industrial growth through its direct effects of (i) limiting competing imports and (ii) providing cheaper scarce inputs to existing manufacturers. It does seem fairly clear that the nature of the licensing system influenced the level of profitability in industries once they were set up, and it may have influenced the choice of industries in which investment took place, but the principal impact of the latter set of forces probably came through the determination of relative input prices rather than relative output prices.

7. SUMMARY—THE GROWTH OF INDIVIDUAL INDUSTRIES

It was possible to identify those variables important to a model of import substitution for a large number of individual industries. These data suggest the following interpretation of the pattern of industrial growth in Pakistan since Partition.

First, the share of domestic markets supplied by domestic production at Partition was very small for a country of Pakistan's size and resource endowment. This was true in virtually all industries for which there is information. Comparison with the Indian structure of production and the exports from India to Pakistan shortly after Partition also suggests strongly that Pakistan would have had a great deal more manufacturing output in most industries had not British India been one economic area. The earliest and most rapid import substitution in Pakistan came in the industries in which India had had significant production and exports to Pakistan, and in which the somewhat smaller size of the Pakistani market did not affect the establishment of efficient size plants.

Second, there were significant declines in the relative prices of many goods in which Pakistan quickly replaced imports. This suggests that the high costs of domestic protection were reduced over a relatively short period of time. In addition, several of the major industries exported a significant share of output by the end of the 1950s, so that prices or costs must have fallen enough to allow profitable exports in those industries.

Third, a principal characteristic of the industries in which import substitution occurred earliest, and which had falling domestic prices, was their low dependence on imported raw materials or their high reliance on domestic raw materials and factors. This is the sort of development that probably would have taken place even if economic policy were neutral. However, the effect of economic policy which drove down the relative price of agricultural raw materials to domestic users provided an additional incentive to users of domestic raw materials, and the tight controls on imports tended to discourage the industries with higher dependence on imports.

Fourth, the tariff structure was differentiated, but the level of tariff protection was significantly associated with the pattern of industrialization only after the source (domestic or imported) of raw materials was accounted for. Even then, the nominal tariff structure was significant in explaining about 10 per cent of the variations in industrial structure, but the effective rate of tariff protection was not associated with the pattern of development in any statistically significant way.

Fifth, data on import licences issued for various goods and to various industries suggest that the stringency of import licensing was related to the prior establishment of domestic manufacturing capacity. The overvaluation of the currency and the import control system combined to make 'all' manufactures scarce in the early and mid-1950s, but the differentially tight licensing of goods came only after domestic manufacturing of particular products began. The import control system did not influence the establishment of industries through making particular goods more scarce and, therefore, more profitable to produce than other goods, at least in the mid-1950s.

Sixth, examination of the extent to which domestic prices exceeded c.i.f. or f.o.b. prices in Pakistan in the mid-1960s indicates that the phase of the import substitution process in the industry was related to the differential between world and domestic prices. In the industries in which the process had been largely completed, the prices domestically were considerably below those implied by the rates of tariff on goods competing with those industries. In the younger industries, domestic prices greatly exceeded the tariff-implied prices, due to the restrictions on competing imports. These latter industries tend to be those in which domestic production was not a dominant share of total supply in the competing industries. There is an intermediate group of industries in which imports are not a significant part of total supply, but prices are well above those implied by tariffs. In some industries this is due to the rapid increase in domestic demand, which has kept ahead of domestic production and resulted in high prices. In other industries, import restrictions on both competing imports and intermediate inputs into the producing industry have restricted supply, and there is excess capacity in the producing industry due to the scarcity of imported inputs.

The evidence on the growth of individual industries is consistent with the view of industrialization that has been proposed throughout the book. The initial disequilibrium caused by Partition and by the trade policy adopted in the 1950s created unusual profit opportunities in domestic manufacturing industries. The industries responded, growing at exceedingly rapid rates throughout the 1950s and 1960s. Differential encouragement of manufacturing industries through tariff and import licensing policy had little effect on the pattern of industrial investment and industrial growth among industries in the 1950s, due to the scarcity of virtually all manufactures and the fact that most of the economic policies adopted merely reinforced the real cost differentials among industries that would have existed even if policy had been neutral. As one moves into the 1960s, however, the differential incentives provided by stringent import licensing of particular goods and more liberal licensing of others, combined with a more highly differentiated tariff structure than existed in the 1950s have tended to make the effects of economic policy much more discriminatory than it was in the 1950s. This is somewhat ironic, since many proponents of the import liberalization of the 1960s argued for liberalization in terms of eliminating the differential effects of economic policy.

CHAPTER VII

An Evaluation of Pakistan's Industrial Growth

The characteristics of economic growth in Pakistan are different in the periods before and after 1959/60, for reasons that have been referred to throughout this book. After summarizing the major conclusions on the relative importance of policy and non-policy determinants of industrial growth in Pakistan I discuss three other aspects of industrialization: the nature of the changes that occurred in economic policy and the structure of growth in the 1960s, some criticisms of the economic structure (and the economic policy) that evolved over the decade of the 1950s, and the evidence on the efficiency of manufacturing industry, and of economic policy, in Pakistan.

1. THE IMPORTANCE OF ECONOMIC POLICY IN THE INDUSTRIALIZATION OF PAKISTAN

The relative importance of economic policy in the industrialization process can be thought of in terms of its effects on the overall rate of growth of manufacturing industry, on the structure of growth among manufacturing industries, and on the incentives for producing (or the relative prices of) manufactured goods. The non-policy variables that were crucial to the development of manufacturing industry in Pakistan were (i) the Partition of the subcontinent in 1947, which destroyed the customs union in which Pakistan was a food and raw material producing area for the rest of India, (ii) the domestic production of agricultural raw materials used in producing the major manufactured goods consumed in Pakistan, (iii) a relatively large market for mass consumption goods, and relatively simple technologies for producing such goods.

I think the evidence is quite clear that the non-policy determinants of differential growth were dominant in the decade up to 1960, though for some industries differential protection to domestic production may have helped in speeding growth. The policy of banning competing imports after domestic production had begun undoubtedly led to marginally more domestic production and less imports than would have been the case in the absence of such restrictive policies. It is important to construct a situation with which the actual experience of growth could be compared. If a scrupulously neutral policy with respect to the exchange rate and with respect to import substitution and export expansion had been adopted, the major difference between actual and hypothetical incentives would not have been among manufacturing industries, but between manufacturing and agriculture. Manufacturing industries that received sanctions to invest also received imported raw materials and capital goods at subsidized prices (given the overvalued currency that existed). Such manufacturers, as well as producers who used agricultural raw materials, were at an advantage relative to anyone who did not receive sanctions and who therefore, had to pay much higher rupee prices for industrial raw materials and for capital goods. A policy of a floating exchange rate would have raised the costs (and probably lowered the output prices) to both kinds of industries, relative to the agricultural producers and to manufacturers not receiving investment and import sanctions. The major impact of economic policy in the 1950s was to transfer income away from agriculture and from urban consumers, and to the new and rapidly growing manufacturing sector. The analysis of implicit exchange rates over time clearly indicates that domestic prices of all categories of manufactured goods were two to three times the c.i.f. prices of such goods at the official exchange rate in the mid-1950s. The general scarcity of manufactures swamped any differential effect the tariff structure might have had in determining relative prices and relative profitabilities in that period.[1]

The abnormally low level of manufacturing activity that Pakistan had at Partition (relative to what one would expect from a country of Pakistan's size and income level) was a major factor in explaining the high overall rate of industrial growth in the 1950s. The other principal factor in the high rate of growth of output was the very high rate of profit in all manufacturing industries provided by the

[1] Indeed, the tariff structure was relatively less differentiated among commodities in the early and mid-1950s than it was in the mid-1960s.

restrictive economic policy adopted at the time of the trade crisis in 1952. Economic policy in the 1950s, however, had little to do with the differential rates of growth and import substitution among manufacturing industries. The differential import substitution, while related in part to differential protection, was primarily associated with differences among industries in the source of their principal raw materials.

By the late 1950s, however, the situation had begun to change. Domestic production supplied a large share of total supply in many industries, particularly those that produced consumption goods. Some manufacturing industries became more and more dependent on artificially cheap sources of imported or domestically produced raw materials. Investors began to look to industries other than those producing the mass consumption goods and using domestic materials. The government-owned and sponsored corporations also began to invest in intermediate goods industries such as paper products and board, cement, fertilizers, and chemicals. The general scarcity of manufactures was eased, and more particular scarcities began to stand out. As opportunities for profitable investment in intermediate goods industries began to emerge with growing domestic markets, a conflict arose between potential producers, who wished to be assured of profitable markets, and existing users of the goods, who did not wish to be cut off from cheap foreign supplies. It became increasingly clear in the late 1950s that a major bottleneck to continued high growth rates of output was the lack of capital goods,[1] and lack of intermediate goods to utilize existing capital goods. The difficulties the economy faced were best analysed by John Power[2] and my interpretation is heavily influenced by his analysis.

The bottleneck that developed in the growth process has three

[1] This problem is discussed by M. Haq, *The Strategy of Economic Planning: A Case Study of Pakistan*, Karachi, 1963; G. F. Papanek, 'Industrial Production and Investment in Pakistan', *Pakistan Development Review*, Autumn 1964; and J. H. Power, 'Industrialization in Pakistan: A Case of Frustrated Take-off?', *Pakistan Development Review*, Summer 1963.

[2] *Ibid.* See also his article, 'Import Substitution as an Industrialization Strategy', *Philippine Economic Journal*, Spring 1967, which develops the theoretical argument more completely.

dimensions to it. First, because of the overvaluation of the currency and the artificially low prices of imported goods, industries adopted technologies that demanded large amounts of foreign capital equipment and of foreign raw materials. An adjustment upward in the price of foreign exchange would have aided in overcoming the bottleneck by changing the 'requirements' of foreign exchange per unit of domestic output. Second, as domestic production of consumption goods substituted for imports, a larger fraction of total foreign exchange earnings became available for importing capital goods and raw materials. There is some indication that industrialists in the late 1950s waited to invest until they could get import licences for capital goods, rather than purchase locally produced capital goods. Maintaining an overvalued currency combined with direct licensing of capital goods imports tended to discourage the domestic production of goods to substitute for certain scarce imports, thus preventing the 'bottleneck' from being overcome by increased domestic production of a substitute good.[1] Finally, because the currency was overvalued, exports both of manufactured goods and of agricultural raw materials were discouraged, so that easing the 'bottleneck' by exporting to purchase imports was also discouraged. For all three reasons, the industrial growth rate began to fall, even though it was respectable by international standards. In addition, the ill effects of squeezing agriculture were felt in the First Plan period, when there was virtually no growth in overall agricultural production. Both the shortage of inputs into agriculture and the lack of incentives given to investment in improved techniques in agriculture took their toll.

Just at the time when the set of policies that had been adopted (including overvaluation of the currency and the differential tariff and import licensing policies) were beginning to inhibit manufacturing growth, a major shift in the availability of foreign exchange relieved the pressure (i) to utilize foreign exchange efficiently and (ii) to reward more highly those domestic resources that earned

[1] One should recall, however, that domestic production of substitute capital and intermediate goods was growing very rapidly. This rapid growth was not enough to overcome the small base from which production started and the other two aspects of the policy distortions mentioned in the text.

foreign exchange. In 1959/60 the increase in the flow of foreign assistance began in full force.[1] Since this occurred simultaneously with an acceleration in the rate of domestic investment, the shortage of foreign exchange continued, and prices of imported raw materials and capital goods continued to exceed their duty-paid prices by wide margins. Aid in the form of increased commodity imports provided greater flows of imports to existing manufacturing industries, and enabled them to utilize installed capacity at a much higher rate than had been possible in the 1950s. The greater availability of foreign exchange also aided in releasing more resources for imports of capital goods, which flowed increasingly into industries producing intermediate and investment goods. Increased supplies of the scarcest resource clearly had the effect of making it less crucial to utilize that resource most efficiently. There were some improvements in the nature of economic policy that accompanied the increased flow of imports, however, and indirect controls bore a larger share of the burden of directing the flow of resources. It was undoubtedly the increased flow of resources, however, that made the system work.

A major question is the extent to which a resumption of high growth rates in manufacturing and the acceleration of growth in other sectors of the economy in the 1960s were due to a change in policy or to changes in other characteristics of the economy. This is too broad a question to be answered satisfactorily here, but some aspects dealing with the manufacturing sector are relevant to this book.

From the data and argument of Chapter IV, it is clear that the liberalization in import controls that occurred in the early 1960s was in part a means of getting the increased supplies of imports absorbed by the economy. Domestic demand for such goods increased so rapidly that the increase in the supply of imports and domestic substitutes did little to depress prices and scarcity margins of the goods until the introduction of the Free List in the last year of the Plan period. The principal effect of the liberalization of imports in the first 4 years of the Second Plan period was to increase the output

[1] The Export Bonus Scheme introduced in 1959 did aid significantly in increasing export earnings but the bulk of the increase in foreign exchange supplied in the succeeding 5 years came from foreign aid.

levels and the level of capacity utilization in industries that were most heavily dependent on imports for raw materials. It also made raw materials more readily available in the small-scale sector of the economy that did not get licences to import directly.[1]

The changes in tariff structure that took place in the Second Plan acted in a different direction. Tariffs became more highly differentiated, and greater incentives were given for import substitution in the consumer goods industries relative to intermediate and capital goods, even though the greatest potential for import substitution existed in the latter industries. In addition, there was little significant change in the incentive given to earning, rather than saving, foreign exchange. Finally, since increased supplies of imports were largely for commodities that already had relatively low duties, the Free List of 1964/65 had the effect of reducing the protection low-duty items had been provided by the licensing system in earlier years. By differentially limiting the effects of the licensing system, there was an increase, rather than a decrease, in the distortions of the protective system in the 1960s. To the extent that the differential system of protection had begun to get the economy into structural difficulties in the late 1950s, the accentuation of these distortions in the mid-1960s increased the likelihood that structural 'bottlenecks' would appear in the future. The increase in imported goods financed by aid put off the day of reckoning for the distorted structure of incentives. The Third Plan recognized that there would be difficulties, and recommended an increase in the level of duties on capital goods. There was an increase in duties introduced in the 1965/66 budget, but the payment of these duties (and, therefore, whatever protective effect that they might have had) was partly suspended shortly after their introduction.

Summarizing, then, the differential effects of the tariff structure, the system of import licensing, and the overvaluation of the currency, had little influence on the structure of production that began to emerge in the mid-1950s, since the scarcity of all manufactured

[1] This change was crucial to the development of tubewell manufacturing and to investment within the agricultural sector in the Second Plan period. See W. P. Falcon and C. H. Gotsch, 'Agricultural Development in Pakistan: Lessons from the Second Plan Period', in G. F. Papanek (ed.), *Development Policy, I*, Cambridge, Mass., 1968.

goods at Partition made it profitable to produce almost any kind of manufacture. The restrictive trade policy speeded the process of industrial growth by transferring substantial amounts of income from the agricultural sector to manufacturers, but it is unlikely that the structure of production would have been very different if, say, a floating exchange rate had been adopted to deal with the exchange crisis in 1952. By the late 1950s, however, the differential effects of economic policy began to be felt, though it is likely that differential policies had more impact on the earnings of foreign exchange than on the structure of domestic manufacturing output. More neutral economic policy, particularly with regard to the exchange rate, probably would have had the principal effect of earning more foreign exchange by the export of some manufactures but particularly through exports of agricultural commodities. The full effects of the policies of differential protection and discrimination against exports were not felt, however, since the increase in imports financed by aid began shortly after shortage of foreign exchange (and the commodities it could purchase) was beginning to affect the rate of growth of manufacturing output and the level of investment. Policy incentives to invest in different industries did not become any less discriminatory in the 1960s, and in fact probably became more unfavourable to the domestic production of certain intermediate goods and capital goods simply because these goods became available to a larger number of users at lower scarcity prices than had been the case earlier. The dangers of differential structure, and of development of industries based on artificially cheap sources of imported raw materials became even greater in the Second Plan period than in the First, though the larger supplies of foreign exchange masked the latter development.

2. ECONOMIC EFFICIENCY AND PAKISTAN'S INDUSTRIAL GROWTH

Two aspects of the economic efficiency of growing industries were discussed in Chapter II. First, under static conditions, what are the differentials in cost of producing goods domestically relative to the costs of importing the same goods? These differentials could be expressed in terms of implicit exchange rates for each good, and distortions in the price or cost structure would be reflected in differentials among implicit exchange rates for various goods. The relative efficiencies of producing different goods could also be expressed as rates of effective protection to each industry, which take into account not only the differential between world and domestic prices of output but also the differentials between world and domestic prices of tradable inputs. The second question related to efficiency brought out in Chapter II was: how have relative costs and prices, or in implicit exchange rates, changed over time as industry developed? Evidence on both aspects of efficiency has been presented earlier, along with evidence on the growth of the various industries in Pakistan. Here the evidence is summarized and is related to information from the other studies of efficiency in the manufacturing sector in Pakistan.

Consider first the evidence on the reduction in cost differentials over time. It is clear from the analysis of implicit exchange rates that the average price of manufactured goods domestically fell relative to world prices in the decade after restrictions were imposed on imports. It is also clear that the average price of agricultural goods domestically rose relative to world price over the same period. The domestic price structure in the years immediately following adoption of trade restrictions had discriminated sharply against the agricultural sector, and the convergences of the average implicit exchange rates for manufacturing and agricultural goods indicated that a major distortion in the domestic price structure was being removed over the period from the early 1950s to the mid-1960s. Over this period, the reductions both in the costs of domestic manufacturers and in the windfalls going to those manufacturers (from being able to buy inputs cheap and sell output dear) were quite substantial. Some additional information on costs has been compiled by Professor Nurul Islam, in a study of Tariff Commission investigations.[1] He found that for twenty of twenty-one manufactured products investigated in at least two time periods, domestic costs had fallen relative to foreign costs. In four industries domestic costs fell by 60 per cent or more relative to c.i.f. prices, while in five more there

[1] N. Islam, *Tariff Protection, Comparative Costs, and Industrialization in Pakistan*, Research Report No. 57, Pakistan Institute of Development Economics, Karachi, 1967.

was a fall of between 40 and 60 per cent. If they are generally representative, these figures suggest that a substantial portion of the decreases in the implicit exchange rates for manufactured goods must have come from cost reductions, rather than from declining profit rates in domestic industries.

Despite the impressive indications of falling costs in domestic infant industries over time, however, there existed in the mid-1960s a substantial amount of economic, if not technical, inefficiency in Pakistan's manufacturing sector. Evidence on this point comes from several sources. Nurul Islam's data from the Tariff Commission studies made in the 1960s showed average costs for domestic manufacturers almost 100 per cent above c.i.f. prices of similar goods.[1] Mallon analysed the implicit multiple exchange rate system that forced raw cotton and jute to receive less than the official exchange price for exports and provided manufacturers of jute and cotton textiles a price of foreign exchange about 30 per cent above the official price.[2] His results suggested a net loss of foreign exchange by the processing industry. At the extreme, the foreign exchange earned by a given quantity of jute exported as textiles was less than the foreign exchange earned by exporting the same jute in raw form.

Finally, a considerable amount of information was presented in earlier chapters on differences between world and domestic relative prices of manufactured goods. These differences are shown for thirty-two industries in Table 36 in the form of average implicit exchange rates for the products of the industries. There is a heavy concentration of rates in a range between 50 and 100 per cent above the official price of foreign exchange, but the range is quite wide. Thirteen of the thirty-two industries had implicit exchange rates more than twice the official exchange rate.

The differences between the implicit exchange rates for inputs (if they are either imported directly by the industrial user or are of domestic agricultural origin) and the implicit rates for output are very wide, so that the degree of effective subsidy to the domestic

[1] N. Islam, *op. cit.* See also his article, 'Comparative Costs, Factor Proportions, and Industrial Efficiency in Pakistan', *Pakistan Development Review*, Summer 1967.

[2] R. D. Mallon, 'Export Policy in Pakistan', *Pakistan Development Review*, Spring 1966.

TABLE 36. *Indicators of the Distortions in the Price of Manufactured Goods in Pakistan*

Industries Producing Primarily	*Domestic Wholesale Value of $1.00 of Product*	*Exchange Rate at which Subsidy to Domestic Industry would be zero*
Consumption Goods		
1. Sugar	14·96	—
2. Edible oils	9·81	—
3. Tea	6·62	4·52
4. Cotton textiles	7·43	15·09
5. Silk and Artificial Silk Textiles	21·42	1137·64
6. Footwear	7·90	7·62
7. Wearing apparel	15.47	99·20
8. Printing and publishing	6·09	5·52
9. Soaps	9·23	13·23
10. Matches	7·72	5·19
11. Plastic goods	15·99	20·80
12. Sports goods	7·62	8·38
13. Pens and Pencils	12·14	13·66
14. Electrical appliances	19·42	63·12
15. Motor vehicles	16·61	—
Intermediate Goods		
16. Jute textiles	6·95	13·47
17. Thread and threadball	8·23	8·71
18. Saw milling	8·23	9·14
19. Tanning	7·43	9·33
20. Rubber products	7·28	29·27
21. Fertilizer	5·47	13·47
22. Paints and varnishes	9·62	10·90
23. Chemicals	8·62	10·23
24. Petroleum products	9·85	4·52
25. Paper products	9·23	11·57
Investment and Related Goods		
26. Non-metallic mineral products	12·09	15·09
27. Cement	8·33	7·19
28. Basic metals	7·90	14·38
29. Metal products	9·28	18·18
30. Non-electrical machinery	9·00	12·85
31. Sewing machinery	7·62	8·66
32. Electrical machinery and equipment	7·62	8·04

Note: Dashes indicate that at no exchange rate would the industry be without subsidy.

Source: Lewis and Guisinger, *op. cit.*

processor is very high. The availability of direct price comparisons for output and for principal inputs made it possible for another study to analyse systematically the difference between the dollar value of output and the dollar value of tradable inputs in each industry.[1] The difference between the two is the value of foreign exchange saved (or earned) by domestic production of the good. Since the actual value added by domestic factors and by inputs of non-traded goods is estimated in the input–output table, one can compute the price of foreign exchange at which the value of domestic factors devoted to production of the good would just equal the foreign exchange earned or saved. This is a slight variation on the procedure of estimating the extent of subsidy or the 'effective rate' of protection given to the domestic industry.[2] The results are also shown in Table 36. The range of exchange rates for the domestic producing industries is much wider than for the goods alone. Only twelve of the thirty-two industries would have no subsidy if the value of foreign exchange was twice the official price, and thirteen industries would still be receiving a subsidy if the value of foreign exchange were three times the official price. The assumption of fixed input coefficients used to make these estimates would not hold true if prices facing producers actually changed.

[1] The 1963/64 input–output table of Tims and Stern was used for the purpose of determining the input structure. The details of the analysis are given in S. R. Lewis and S. E. Guisinger, 'Measuring Protection in a Developing Country: The Case of Pakistan', *Journal of Political Economy*, 1968.

[2] In a simple case where all inputs except primary factors are tradable, the multiple of the exchange rate at which the value added at domestic prices would equal the value added at world prices is found by solving for q in the following expression (which is drawn from equation 2.10):

$$W_i = q \left\{ \frac{X_i}{1 + t_i} - \sum_j \frac{X_{ji}}{1 + t_j} \right\}$$

W_i is value added at domestic prices and the expression in brackets is the difference between the value of output at world prices and the value of tradable inputs at world prices. The implicit exchange rates observed in 1963/64, rather than the tariff rates, were used in the calculations made by Lewis and Guisinger, *op. cit.*, and reported in Table 36. The relationship between this factor and the rate of effective protection is worked out in Lewis and Guisinger.

Undoubtedly many of these industries would be socially profitable at an exchange rate considerably lower than the levels suggested by these figures because of the possibilities of substitution. Even if they are only of the right order of magnitude, however, it is clear that substantial distortions still existed in the mid-1960s, in domestic prices as guides to social opportunity costs. Given the evidence that the distortions, particularly in manufactured relative to agricultural goods prices, narrowed over the decade 1954–64, one can imagine the extent of the distortions that existed in the earlier period.

Another method of utilizing the direct price comparisons, besides computing the value of foreign exchange at which the industry would become socially profitable, is to compute the share of value added at domestic prices that is 'due to' the distortions of the price structure of tradable goods. This calculation was also made by Lewis and Guisinger.[1] The computation suggested that one-half to two-thirds of actual value added by domestic manufacturers was the result of the distortions in the price structure. The most disturbing aspect of this result is that some of the older and more well-established industries suffer from high degrees of inefficiency. Over two-thirds of the value added in jute and cotton textiles, for example, were 'due to' the fact that the industry buys its principal input at less than the official price of foreign exchange (due to an export tax) and sells it for considerably more than the official price (due to the Export Bonus Scheme). If the firms in the industry were required to buy and sell at the same price for foreign exchange, there would probably be two results. First, some firms would probably become unprofitable, though the number would most likely be small in these two industries. Second, there would be substantial drop in the rate of profit in the industries, and they would most certainly become less attractive for potential investors.

The data on which the analysis of effective subsidies is based are not sufficient to determine the extent to which there is 'over-industrialization' in Pakistan, or the extent to which there is just an abundance of profit and a sizable transfer of income to manufacturers. If the analysis of industrial growth up to the 1960s is correct, however, it is unlikely that there is 'over-industrialization' in the aggregate. There would definitely be a reallocation of investment

[1] *Op. cit.*

within manufacturing if a less distorted set of relative prices were given to the economy. Some manufacturers would definitely go out of business, which would be a very healthy event for the economy. Other manufacturing activities that were discouraged by government policies would become much more attractive. There would undoubtedly be a flow of investment resources into some branches of the machinery and electrical equipment and other metal-working industries if a more neutral policy was adopted with regard to the pricing of foreign exchange.

One advantage that Pakistan had in the 1950s is disappearing. When all manufactured goods were exeedingly scarce, there was little that could go wrong with a policy of producing whatever appeared most profitable. The more that domestic productive capacity expanded, however, the greater became the costs of misallocation. Pakistan reached a point in the mid-1960s at which she should have looked to more traditional criteria of efficiency for investment decisions. The distortions in the prices of manufactured goods were still so great that private profitability was virtually no guide at all to social profitability. The direction of the 'import liberalization' policy of the Second Plan, which was to reduce the domestic scarcities of those goods on which the tariffs were already low, made it increasingly unprofitable to produce domestically the goods that were being used at a subsidized price by domestic manufacturing industries. While John Power's analysis of the distorted structure of manufacturing industry and the fruits it would reap in future growth potential turned out to be a bit wide of the mark in the late 1950s and early 1960s, the direction of major policies in the mid-1960s increased the likelihood that private investment decisions would be inconsistent with social priorities.

Economists with a bias in favour of efficient static resource allocation criteria can easily see the costs of current and past economic policies in Pakistan. Inefficient present uses of foreign exchange and capital abound, as indicated by Table 36 and other sources in this monograph. Present distortions make it privately less profitable to 'break bottlenecks' that now exist, particularly with regard to efficient choice of import substituting and exporting industries. The distortions between implicit exchange rates for inputs and for output increase the danger of adopting techniques that are inappropriate both to Pakistan's factor endowment and to world opportunity costs for tradable inputs and output. Finally, some of the income distribution effects of protected industrialization are viewed as unfortunate by those concerned with equitable distribution of the increments to GNP. Regional inequalities in *per capita* income widened from 1950 to 1965 and scattered evidence on the consumption of goods with high income elasticities of demand indicate that the small gains in *per capita* income that were achieved were received by those with already high incomes.

The benefit side of the industrialization policies are also impressive, however. Certainly a part of the 15 per cent per year growth rate of manufacturing value added can be credited to conscious policy rather than to the effects of Partition. The diversification of export structure had been impressive, and it is closely related to policy changes. Pakistan's ability to break new industries into exports is conspicuous among major developing countries. A counterpart of the unfortunate income distribution aspects of industrialization seems to have been the sharp rise in the saving rate, due to the reinvestment of profits, though it is not easy to document this point. Finally, through a combination of (i) increased flows of foreign assistance, (ii) increased government investment programs, and (iii) policies that stimulated private investment activity, the government of Pakistan managed to accelerate the pace of change and modernization so that by the mid-1960s a momentum had been reached that would be hard to stop.

The major distortions in price structure due to economic policy in the 1950s were productive, on balance, in terms of economic growth. The continuation of the distortions into the 1960s began to run risks of greater losses from static inefficiency than gains from increased growth. Unless the distortions that existed in the mid-1960s are sharply reduced, it is unlikely that Pakistan will reduce the deficit in her balance of payments without seriously jeopardizing the growth of real income.

APPENDIX—DATA AND SOURCES

The data that appear in the text are drawn from a variety of sources, including published and unpublished official figures of the government of Pakistan and its various agencies and ministries, and the published and unpublished primary collections of data from the Pakistan Institute of Development Economics. The introduction given here is to aid those who wish to pursue matters further. Detailed descriptions of the data and methods are given in several individual studies which preceded this monograph, or in the work of other staff members of the Pakistan Institute of Development Economics. The following sections deal briefly with the data on industrial output, imports, exports and indirect tax collections; indirect tax rates and methods for calculating protection; prices and implicit exchange rates for manufactured and agricultural goods; and licensing of private imports into Pakistan.

1. INDUSTRIAL STRUCTURE DATA

There are several sources of data on industrial output in Pakistan. A *Census of Manufacturing Industries* was begun in 1953, and has been published for 1954, 1955, 1957, 1958, and 1959/60.[1] Compilations for 1962/63 and 1963/64 are in process. The Census deals with what is called 'large-scale' manufacturing in Pakistan. This includes establishments registered under section 2(j) of the Factories Act, that is, those which employed twenty or more persons on any day of the Census year and used power in their operations. Since not all factories meeting this definition are in fact registered, and since there is a downward bias to all reporting for tax purposes, it is desirable to have alternative checks on the output and value added estimates given in the Census.[2] Independent evidence on physical output in a number of industries is given by trade associations and by the Central

[1] The Census of Manufacturing Industries is published by the Central Statistical Office, Karachi.

[2] For a discussion of biases in the Census, see G. F. Papanek, 'Industrial Production and Investment in Pakistan', *Pakistan Development Review*, Autumn 1964.

Board of Revenue from its data on excisable goods' production.[1] In addition, there are data on the collection of sales taxes by the Central Board of Revenue, and since the *ad valorem* rates of sales tax are known, one can imply the value of output in an industry if one knows the collections of sales taxes from that industry. For many industries, it is possible to make alternative estimates of output from all three methods, and to compare the results. The coverage of sales and excise taxes is not precisely on establishments registered under section 2(j) of the Factories Act, but the tax laws do exempt smaller establishments from payment of taxes. In general, where several output estimates of reasonable derivation were available, the highest one was chosen, in order to correct for the downward bias in all the reporting systems due to the desire to avoid tax payments. In addition to these methods and sources, the input–output table for 1963/64 constructed by W. Tims and J. J. Stern[2] provides estimates of output for all the industries covered in this study. The methods used for each of the estimates in 1954/55, 1959/60, and 1963/64 are described in detail in the Appendix to Lewis and Soligo, 'Growth and Structural Change in Pakistan's Manufacturing Industry'.[3]

In this monograph, data for 1951/52 have been added in order to examine the structural changes that preceded the First Plan period. The basic procedure used for all industries was to accept the 1954/55 figure for gross value of output, and project the value of output back to 1951/52 using (i) physical output indices published by the Central Statistical Office, and (ii) price indices from Lewis and Hussain, *Relative Price Changes and Industrialization in Pakistan*.[4] Value added was derived by assuming the ratio of gross value added to gross value of output had not changed since 1954/55. Since physical output series on most industries (in terms of number) were not

[1] These data are published by the Central Statistical Office, Karachi, in the various issues of its monthly *Statistical Bulletin*, and the *Pakistan Statistical Yearbook*.

[2] This table appears as an Appendix to *The Methodology of Estimating Import Requirements*, International Economics Section, Planning Commission, mimeographed, 1965.

[3] *Pakistan Development Review*, Spring 1965.

[4] Monograph No. 16, Pakistan Institute of Development Economics, Karachi, 1967.

available, only eleven industries were included in 1951/52, but they contributed approximately three-fourths of industrial value added in all industries in 1954/55.

Four industries for which output and value added were reported by the Census of Manufacturing Industries were omitted from the analysis and from re-estimation of output and value added for large-scale manufacturing: wheat milling, rice husking, jute pressing and baling, and cotton ginning. All four industries have very low ratios of value added to gross output, and the reported output and value added data in the Censuses are of dubious reliability. This latter is due to (i) the seasonal nature and (ii) the small size of the establishments in the industries. In addition, grain milling and rice husking must always be done, and it is reasonably clear that a large part of the growth in these industries since Partition is due to the substitution of output of large-scale for the output of small-scale enterprises.

In addition to gross value and the gross value of output at factor cost, there are four other sets of data necessary from each industry in order to make the analysis of changing industrial structure: indirect taxes on domestic production, indirect taxes on imports, imports c.i.f. and exports f.o.b. Indirect tax collections are necessary to convert output at factor cost and imports c.i.f. to output and imports at market price. Unless such a correction is made, it is misleading to add imports and domestic production in order to find total supply of the goods of an industry. Presumably the goods compete with one another at market prices, including all indirect taxes. The indirect tax data were unpublished data kindly supplied by the Statistical Office of the Central Board of Revenue. Import and export data come from the published sources of the Central Statistical Office, principally the various issues of the *Pakistan Statistical Yearbook*, the *Statistical Bulletin*, and the *Foreign Trade Statistics of Pakistan*. Again, more precise information on the methods used can be found in the Appendix to Lewis and Soligo, 'Growth and Structural Change in Pakistan's Manufacturing Industry.'

Some objection has been raised to (i) the methods used in calculating the output of the various industries and (ii) the division of the industries into those producing primarily consumption goods, intermediate goods, and investment and related goods.[1] My response to the first criticism has already been published elsewhere,[2] but it is basically that the estimates were a reasonable set of alternative numbers that raised some questions about the value added estimates then in general use, and that the upward corrections of output in many industries were thoroughly justified. In addition, the results of the analysis of structural change were not challenged by the questioning of the output data.

Since some of the conclusions of this monograph regarding the interpretation of structural change do rest on the distinctions drawn between industries producing goods of different types, the criticism of the industrial classification does bear some mention. Winston and MacEwan argued that reclassifying industries on the basis of the 1963/64 input–output table's destination of their output leads one to conclude that the structural change was much less sharp than indicated in the text here and in the Lewis and Soligo paper, 'Growth and Structural Change in Pakistan's Manufacturing Industry'. The principal reasons why I do not accept this criticism are the following: (i) The use of the 1963/64 inter-industry deliveries for adjusting the 1954/55 output is not demonstrably more accurate in explaining the output of particular kinds of goods than the method of classifying industries by 'primary' destination of product. (ii) In the particular adjustment that Winston and MacEwan made, they accepted the input–output table's values uncritically, even where the table indicated that over three-fourths of jute textile output went to consumption uses, which quite clearly makes little sense. Correcting this anomaly, one finds that much of the difference disappears between the Winston/MacEwan estimates of industrial structure and the Lewis/Soligo estimates,[3] especially in the relative importance of intermediate and consumption goods.

The basic industrial data are given in Tables A-1 to A-4 for the 4 years included in the analysis.

[1] The former point was raised by G. F. Papanek, 'Growth and Structural Change in Pakistan's Manufacturing Industry: Comment', *Pakistan Development Review*, Winter 1965. The latter was raised in G. C. Winston and A. MacEwan, 'A Note on the Use-Classification of Four-Digit Industries', *Pakistan Development Review*, Winter 1966.

[2] 'Reply', with R. Soligo, *Pakistan Development Review*, Winter 1966.

2. INDIRECT TAX AND TARIFF RATES

Several sources were used for information on indirect tax rates. The Central Board of Revenue provided an unpublished statement of excise duties over time. Various issues of the *Pakistan Customs Tariff* and the *Annual Customs and Excise Administration Report*[1] were used for import and export duties. Sales tax information was taken from Butt's *The Law of Sales Tax*[2] and the *Report of the Sales Tax Committee.*[3] Specific duties were converted to *ad valorem* by calculating the implied *ad valorem* rates from wholesale prices (inclusive of duties) as reported in the *Statistical Yearbook* of the Central Statistical Office.

Simple averages of tax rates were used in all computations. Such a procedure can easily be criticized, but appropriate weights are difficult to arrive at. Imports would clearly be an inferior weighting system due to the protectionist policy, and there are no detailed data on domestic production, so net availability, or total supply, could not be used either. In view of the large number of commodities involved in most heterogeneous industries or categories, however, the simple unweighted averages probably give a fairly appropriate measure of average tariff and tax levels for purposes of studying incentive structure for import substitution.

[1] These are publications of the Central Board of Revenue.
[2] M. Butt and M. Saeed, *The Law of the Sales Tax*, Lahore, 1964.
[3] Central Board of Revenue, Karachi, 1962.

---

[3] The percentage distribution of gross output among industry groups under three methods of allocating were as follows (1963/64)

	Lewis/ Soligo (%)	*Winston/ MacEwan* (%)	*Winston/MacEwan Adjusted for Jute Goods* (%)
Consumption	59·8	71·6	66·1
Intermediate	20·3	13·9	19·1
Investment	20·7	14·8	14·8

TABLE A-1. *Summary Statistics by Industry, 1951/52 (Current Prices, Rs. '000)*

No.	*Industry Name*	*Gross Value Added*	*Gross Output at Factor Cost*	*Domestic Indirect Taxes*	*Imports c.i.f.*	*Import Taxes*	*Exports Adjusted for Bonus Receipts*
2070	Sugar manufacturing	25,508	85,878	3,000	229,886	71,817	—
2091	Edible oils	5,705	43,582	3,962	24,422	2,815	—
2092	Tea manufacturing	1,996	45,027	2,500	1,456	2,512	30,621
2200	Tobacco manufacturing	21,229	42,277	15,100	6,100	1,284	—
2311, 2390, 2490	Cotton and other textiles	79,363	178,106	18,338	956,900	196,016	2,820
2313	Jute textiles	1,204	2,417	320	43,796	5,343	446
3000	Rubber and rubber goods	2,853	7,328	384	14,599	8,024	—
3191	Matches	1,333	1,851	600	6,000	14,051	—
3300	Non-metallic minerals	21,942	50,207	1,543	11,381	1,553	—
3200	Petrol and coal manufacturing	24,711	62,397	16,300	98,527	72,913	—
3400	Basic metals						
3500	Metal products	16,823	54,431	190	272,159	57,112	—
TOTAL	11 industries	202,667	573,501	62,237	1,665,226	433,440	33,887

TABLE A-2. *Summary Statistics by Industry, Average of 1954 and 1955 (Current Prices, Rs. '000)*

No.	*Industry Name*	*Gross Value Added*	*Gross Output at Factor Cost*	*Domestic Indirect Taxes*	*Imports c.i.f.*	*Import Taxes*	*Exports Adjusted for Bonus Receipts*
2070	Sugar manufacturing	31,420	97,576	11,912	56,207	54,474	—
2091	Edible oils	11,798	92,175	6,448	4,157	501	—
2092	Tea manufacturing	5,760	132,415	5,075	1,157	2,132	40,597
2099	Food manufacturing, NEC	8,732	19,447	25,483	14,355	2,702	809
2100	Beverages	8,645	17,938	3,322	1,409	7,195	3
2200	Tobacco manufacturing	36,537	72,639	26,237	655	846	11
2311, 2390, 2490	Cotton and other textiles	289,327	631,721	84,600	102,069	75,394	6,126
2313	Jute textiles	38,344	83,720	3,446	517	—	49,020
2314	Silk and artificial silk textiles	19,250	35,256	2,885	24,540	26,040	—
2420	Footwear	18,653	40,200	672	—	82	n.a.
2500	Wood and Furniture	1,251	3,291	353	5,161	1,755	273
2600							
2700	Paper manufacturing	12,811	30,503	1,488	22,477	10,240	30
2800	Printing and publishing	20,738	37,164	—	3,660	—	208
2900	Leather manufacturing	11,254	37,021	366	374	38	32,366
3000	Rubber and rubber goods	5,442	13,273	1,425	11,612	9,584	9
3114	Fertilizer	658	2,848	—	11,370	—	5,332
3150	Soap, perfumes, etc.	8,479	23,750	1,731	3,904	892	23
3191	Matches	18,852	27,683	6,987	278	816	—
3199	Chemicals and pharmaceuticals	16,145	36,280	2,405	86,144	6,995	3,974
3200	Petroleum and coal manufacturing	31,155	71,951	27,112	108,182	76,372	10,326
3300	Non-metallic mineral manufacturing	29,056	64,000	4,444	15,052	1,450	427
3400	Basic metal industries	14,105	50,656	726	106,591	19,276	45
3500	Metal products	18,624	54,927	575	9,447		1,808
3600	Machinery except electrical	7,479	16,959	—	232,998	16,839	1,201
3700	Electrical machinery and equipment	5,607	12,657	1,281	47,231	7,376	161
3800	Transport equipment	8,543	18,653	11	83,059	31,358	1,187
3900	Miscellaneous manufacturing industries	10,743	19,014	787	35,242	2,783	5,802
TOTAL	Manufacturing	689,408	1,743,087	219,771	987,848	355,140	159,738

Source: Appendix A of Lewis and Soligo, *op. cit.*

TABLE A-3. *Summary Statistics by Industry, 1959/60 (Current Prices, Rs. '000)*

No.	*Industry Name*	*Gross Value Added*	*Gross Output at Factor Cost*	*Domestic Indirect Taxes*	*Imports c.i.f.*	*Import Taxes*	*Exports Adjusted for Bonus Receipts*
2070	Sugar manufacturing	59,998	190,470	24,500	19	7	4,496
2091	Edible oils	28,322	211,355	21,682	7,082	1,088	—
2092	Tea manufacturing	18,640	147,935	7,700	896	88	35,490
2099	Food manufacturing, NEC	21,981	63,347	25,895	29,543	2,543	11,493
2100	Beverages	8,887	18,438	3,152	3,430	9,678	3
2200	Tobacco manufacturing	81,739	168,187	50,700	397	533	175
2311, 2390, 2490	Cotton and other textiles	586,961	1,428,129	192,298	27,737	16,613	310,341
2313	Jute textiles	173,071	369,021	6,871	41	—	300,311
2314	Silk and artificial silk textiles	40,583	80,046	1,346	37,428	40,703	7
2420	Footwear	29,918	71,404	2,890	—	165	n.a.
2500	Wood and furniture	6,925	13,318	1,058	527	2,486	277
2600							
2700	Paper manufacturing	34,012	82,957	3,341	36,426	6,840	964
2800	Printing and publishing	36,942	63,366	—	7,899	—	1,081
2900	Leather manufacturing	32,262	163,755	271	1,716	131	161,045
3000	Rubber and rubber goods	12,608	25,216	2,327	37,895	15,738	365
3114	Fertilizer	5,187	18,263	—	25,326	—	9,984
3150	Soap, perfumes, etc.	32,805	91,890	14,015	5,580	954	877
3191	Matches	28,260	39,414	18,700	—	—	—
3199	Chemicals and pharmaceuticals	68,995	135,285	6,720	209,624	9,440	13,909
3200	Petroleum and coal manufacturing	52,405	116,455	44,700	240,017	90,665	17,423
3300	Non-metallic mineral manufacturing	81,713	157,908	7,336	42,730	3,888	935
3400	Basic metal industries	39,165	100,680	1,125	257,146	26,385	1,234
3500	Metal products	60,090	152,126	1,207	41,679		7,094
3600	Machinery except electrical	32,540	70,740	—	444,604	40,547	1,114
3700	Electrical machinery and equipment	28,588	67,745	4,241	150,420	14,970	61
3800	Transport equipment	45,357	119,047	1,121	183,155	45,169	11,963
3900	Miscellaneous manufacturing industries	26,504	44,922	1,289	70,496	6,781	30,791
TOTAL	Manufacturing	1,674,458	4,211,419	444,585	1,861,756	335,412	921,433

Source: See Appendix A of Lewis and Soligo, *op. cit.*

TABLE A-4. *Summary Statistics by Industry, 1963/64 (Current Prices, Rs. '000)*

No.	*Industry Name*	*Gross Value Added*	*Gross Output at Factor Cost*	*Domestic Indirect Taxes*	*Imports c.i.f.*	*Import Taxes*	*Exports Adjusted for Bonus Receipts*
2070	Sugar manufacturing	108,242	383,835	76,400	1,670	702	10,636
2091	Edible oils	63,747	574,294	43,457	164,570	6,576	17,321
2092	Tea manufacturing	30,986	183,351	31,800	1,690	1,047	22
2099	Food manufacturing, NEC	28,981	64,260	17,012	41,022	10,822	14,781
2100	Beverages	11,640	26,055	39,660	5,738	14,730	145
2200	Tobacco manufacturing	253,168	404,422	105,994	755	882	3,524
2311, 2390, 2490	Cotton and other textiles	806,138	2,010,320	214,332	45,196	27,529	249,609
2313	Jute textiles	217,507	517,874	16,446	—	—	461,480
2314	Silk and artificial silk textiles	55,709	105,509	985	62,722	66,638	245
2420	Footwear	39,920	86,220	3,530	719	—	19,445
2500	Wood and furniture	13,147	20,010	1,769	17,159	8,973	468
2600							
2700	Paper manufacturing	70,317	158,730	13,116	48,010	18,449	9,838
2800	Printing and publishing	69,589	119,160	—	12,734	—	583
2900	Leather manufacturing	48,432	189,930	660	3,531	11,900	147,442
3000	Rubber and rubber goods	21,386	42,265	2,702	77,489	23,818	4,835
3114	Fertilizer	28,280	80,569	—	26,036	—	45,089
3150	Soap, perfumes, etc.	39,540	110,671	24,323	12,641	5,987	14,852
3191	Matches	33,623	47,490	24,000	—	—	—
3199	Chemicals and pharmaceuticals	137,115	261,670	14,869	358,766	67,053	26,800
3200	Petroleum and coal manufacturing	108,383	223,010	241,435	200,606	112,382	7,503
3300	Non-metallic mineral manufacturing	159,267	250,420	43,792	127,443	24,609	5,452
3400	Basic metal industries	178,392	408,220	12,940	618,293	168,751	13,275
3500	Metal products	145,876	291,920	6,745	131,495		
3600	Machinery except electrical	82,167	165,660	—	807,527	101,621	8,514
3700	Electrical machinery and equipment	95,824	180,460	17,066	255,457	110,409	7,252
3800	Transport equipment	67,306	207,737	3,179	478,582	179,217	18,133
3900	Miscellaneous manufacturing industries	79,805	138,310	2,061	75,041	28,979	66,578
TOTAL	Manufacturing	2,994,494	7,252,372	932,218	3,574,892	991,074	1,153,822

Source: See Appendix A of Lewis and Soligo, *op. cit.*

Rates of effective protection were calculated for 1954/55 and for 1963/64 on the basis of a 1963/64 input–output table constructed by Tims and Stern, following the formulas given in the Chapter II text. Calculations were done at the Pakistan Institute of Development Economics by G. M. Radhu. The method used to arrive at the U_is was different from that of the already published Soligo and Stern results, which deflated output at market price by tariffs.[1] If 'tariffs'

TABLE A-5. *Percentage Rates of Nominal Tariff, Nominal Protection, and Implicit Protection in Pakistan, 1954/55 and 1963/64*

	1954/55			*1963/64*				
	t_i	$t_i - t_{ai}$	U_i	t_i	$t_i - t_{ai}$	U_i	$\frac{S/S_1}{U_i}$	$\frac{S/S_2}{U_i}$
Consumption Goods								
Canning	49	42	78	112	105	265	311	311
Bakery products	50	50	55	107	92	89	121	120
Sugar refining	63	58	170	62	55	109	115	87
Edible oils	46	40	106	47	45	100	202	155
Tea	18	14	22	14	−2	−60	45	−35
Salt	71	0	−8	100	38	40	78	−15
Non-alcoholic beverages	90	72	88	107	81	90	108	−6
Cigarettes	131	98	94	175	207	106	130	118
Cotton textiles	76	58	103	159	127	147	152	135
Woollen textiles	45	35	49	164	139	144	146	142
Silk and artificial silk textiles	125	98	93	200	174	121	141	139
Knitting	64	54	46	170	155	94	130	130
Footwear	46	43	47	91	76	76	104	94
Wearing apparel	55	45	33	230	223	161	217	216
Wood products	43	36	226	96	81	269	184	318
Printing and publishing	0	0	−17	0	0	−13	−15	−15
Leather goods	64	54	57	100	92	80	112	85
Soaps, cosmetics	49	36	−13	73	35	1	64	11
Matches	132	97	91	95	33	38	92	59
Optical goods	43	33	25	49	34	67	31	24
Plastic goods	51	41	40	107	94	81	77	75
Sports goods	75	75	74	72	72	67	48	48
Pencils and pens	66	51	44	61	46	39	39	33

[1] R. Soligo and J. J. Stern, 'Tariff Protection, Import Substitution and Investment Efficiency', *Pakistan Development Review*, Summer 1965; and 'Reply to Papanek', *Pakistan Development Review*, Spring 1966.

	1954/55			*1963/64*				
	t_i	$t_i - t_{di}$	U_i	t_i	$t_i - t_{di}$	U_i	$\frac{S/S_1}{U_i}$	$\frac{S/S_2}{U_i}$
Intermediate Goods								
Jute textiles	48	38	63	70	51	92	152	145
Dyeing and printing	43	33	−44	130	115	90	138	138
Threadball	49	39	21	92	84	62	145	145
Saw milling	30	30	64	61	61	157	152	152
Tanning	26	16	28	61	61	160	211	211
Rubber products	51	40	72	41	25	39	81	59
Fertilizers	0	0	43	0	0	28	18	123
Paints/varnishes	43	33	46	49	23	27	46	12
Chemicals and pharmaceuticals	34	28	60	33	24	−10	33	51
Petroleum and coal products	40	25	46	57	−23	−55	101	92
Paper products	46	39	61	77	62	83	59	78
Investment and Related Goods								
Metal furniture	43	33	117	130	115	268	253	253
Non-metallic minerals	93	80	67	69	49	46	46	29
Cement	49	39	40	69	38	33	58	29
Basic metals	24	18	20	17	9	3	58	56
Metal products	48	41	83	66	59	247	98	93
Non-electrical machinery	5	5	−5	12·5	12·5	14	11	11
Sewing machines	54	54	92	85	85	120	78	78
Electrical goods	79	59	14	104	82	75	67	59
Electrical machinery	19	19	66	22	22	20	25	11
Other transport equipment	14	14	14	20	20	26	33	34
Motor vehicles	80	70	280	93	78	292	396	394
Cycles	41	41	103	92	92	182	161	161

Note: T_i is used when U_i is negative.

Sources: See Appendix text for methods and sources. S/S_1 and S/S_2 are the two sets of estimates given by Soligo and Stern, the first deflating output at factor cost by tariffs, the second deflating output at market price by tariffs.

included all taxes on imports this would be a proper result, but they used only the tariff rates and not sales taxes on imports. We deflated output at factor cost by nominal tariff (including sales taxes on imports) minus domestic indirect taxes. Inputs were deflated by nominal tariffs including sales taxes on imports. We also corrected for the subsidy to domestic users of raw cotton and raw jute that is inherent in the export duty on these goods. The results could differ for several reasons, therefore. The Soligo–Stern results for 1963/64 are compared with our results in Table A-5 where we have shown nominal tariff, nominal protection, and our value of U_i for 1954/55 and for 1963/64 as well as the two separate Soligo–Stern results for the latter year.

The two Soligo–Stern results differ in a predictable manner. Since they deflated a large measure of output (at market price rather than at factor cost) by the same tariff rate, their second set of calculations showed somewhat lower rates of protection for virtually all industries than the results of their original article. Our results are more comparable to their second set of results, and the differences in methods are fairly obvious. Where sales taxes were important on imports (e.g. metal products, beverages, optical goods, plastic goods, sports goods, pencils and pens) our measure shows greater protection. Our measure is generally close to their second measure or somewhat less than it. In either of their methods or ours, the extent to which nominal rates understate effective rates for various industries is clear-cut again.

In general, the relations of nominal to effective protection for the forty-six industries in Table A–5 is approximately the same as for the twenty-seven industries considered in the text: nominal rates are a reasonable guide to effective rates, with fairly predictable exceptions.

The interpretation placed on the results was very different in Soligo and Stern from what was suggested here. Soligo and Stern point out that a U_i in excess of 100 per cent implies that value at free trade prices is negative. That is, the value of inputs at world prices exceeds the value of output at world prices. Thus, they conclude that the investment in these industries is inefficient to a startling degree. All we have tried to show here, however, is that the tariff and tax structure is arranged in such a way that value added in an industry *could* be negative if prices reflected tariff and tax rates only. This conclusion should not be startling in view of the very high rates of nominal protection.

In the text and appendix tables, U_i is used as the measure of effective protection where protection is positive, and T_i is used when effective protection is negative. The reason is that T_i is distinctly non-linear when protection is positive, it approaches infinity as $\hat{W}_i$ approaches zero, then starts from negative infinity as $\hat{W}_i$ becomes negative, and approaches -1 as $\hat{W}_i$ falls below zero. U_i makes more meaningful comparison in the range of protection found in Pakistan. For negative protection, however, since U_i is non-linear and approaches negative infinity as $\hat{W}_i$ exceeds W_i, while T_i is linear in that range, T_i has been used.

3. PRICES AND IMPLICIT EXCHANGE RATES

For a more complete discussion of the sources of data and methods of calculation used in constructing the price and implicit exchange rate indices, the reader should refer to Lewis, 'Effects of Trade Policy on Domestic Relative Prices: Pakistan, 1951–1964,'[1] and Lewis and Hussain, *Relative Price Changes and Industrialization in Pakistan.*[2] Only a brief description is given here.

The domestic prices used were average annual wholesale prices, and were simple averages of several geographic centres or markets in each province. These data were generally found in the publications of the Central Statistical Office, although the Institute of Development Economics monograph, *A Measure of Inflation in Pakistan*[3] was also used as a source. Occasionally, where necessary, the price index was interpolated using an index of retail prices. The consumption goods prices and the agricultural crop prices are the best quality and reflect the trends in prices most effectively. Livestock prices are not particularly good, nor are the price indices for some intermediate or investment goods. In calculating the terms of trade between sectors, it might have been more appropriate to use retail prices for purchases and harvest prices for sales of the agricultural sector, but this was rejected for two reasons. First, retail price data are available only for urban centres, and are thought to be generally less reliable than wholesale price data. Second, only wholesale price data are comparable with c.i.f. or f.o.b. prices that were used in the study of implicit exchange rates between domestic and 'world' prices. To ensure comparability between the two parts of the study wholesale prices were used domestically. Where there were both free market and controlled prices averages were used, since both prices represent transactions in segmented markets and are likely to overstate and understate, respectively, the scarcity price of the good in

[1] *American Economic Review,* March 1968. [2] *Op. cit.*
[3] Monograph No. 4, Karachi, 1961.

question. While this is unsatisfactory from a theoretical point of view, it is unlikely that there is any systematic bias in the results because of the decision.

Weighting systems for price indices were chosen because of the interest in the terms of trade between the two sectors. Because of international trade (and the presence domestically of other sectors) the purchases of one sector are not equal to the sales of any single other sector. For this reason the terms of trade of the agricultural sector are not simply the reciprocal of the terms of trade of the non-agricultural sector, even if the same prices are used in both calculations. Several different weighting schemes were used for each sector. Production, value added, and net domestic availability were all tried as weights. Since actual transactions between sectors are not recorded anywhere, and since no estimates of such transactions have been made, many decisions on sales and purchase weights were educated guesses. The weighting alternatives finally used are given in the Appendix to Lewis and Hussain for each commodity included in the study for East and West Pakistan separately. Fortunately, the results of the relative price analysis were not particularly sensitive to the choice of the weighting system.

The data on which the implicit exchange rates are based are somewhat less reliable than those for domestic prices alone. Sources are different for agricultural and for manufactured goods, and are different among manufactured goods as well. A brief description of the sources and methods is given here.[1]

The basic sources for 'world' prices of agricultural goods were the various issues of the FAO *Production Yearbook* and *Trade Yearbook*. Prices for major exporting countries or from major importing countries or commercial centres, in U.S. dollars, were obtained from those sources, and were adjusted for freight charges. Because of the greater standardization and the fact that price data, not unit value data, were available, the movements of 'world' agricultural prices are probably more reliable over time than those for manufactured goods.[2]

The implicit exchange rates for manufactured goods were generally

[1] The next five paragraphs are adapted from my article 'Effects of Trade Policy . . .', *op. cit.*

[2] Agricultural commodities covered in the study were: coarse, medium, and fine rice, wheat, maize, barley, sorghum, pulses (lentils), potatoes,

estimated for 1964, and implicit rates for earlier years were estimated by projecting backwards using the domestic price indices from Lewis and Hussain and international price indices described below. The methods for estimating the implicit rate were of two basic types. One was based on direct price comparisons of the sort used for agricultural goods. The basic source for the direct price comparisons was the import price surveys reported by *Pal.*[1] For any industry in which imports were a substantial proportion of total supply, the implicit rate for imports competing with that industry was used as the implicit exchange rate for the industry as a whole. The reasoning is that for those industries, the price of competing imports determines the domestic market price for both imports and for domestic production.

In the second group of industries where exports are a substantial part of total supply, and where the products in the industry are sufficiently homogeneous, the export price is a good representation of the ex-factory price of the goods the industry produces. Since the exchange rate (including bonus vouchers) at which the industry exports is known, if one assumes that the producers equate prices in the two markets, domestic and international, then the implicit exchange rate between producers' prices and world prices is given by the exchange rate for exports.[2]

[1] M. L. Pal, 'The Determinants of the Domestic Prices of Imports', *Pakistan Development Review*, Winter 1964, and 'Domestic Prices of Imports: Extension of Empirical Findings', *Pakistan Development Review*, Winter 1965. These studies were detailed comparisons between import prices c.i.f. and the wholesale prices in the port cities of Karachi and Chittagong.

[2] If producers were less than perfect competitors domestically (which would be true for such things as paper), then they would not equate price but marginal revenue in the two markets, and the export rate would understate the implicit exchange rate. In view of the interest in the size of the difference between the rate for manufactures and for agricultural products, the fact that the method may have understated the exchange rates for some commodities, particularly cotton textiles, simply means that the differentials between world and domestic prices or terms of trade are greater than the estimates suggest. The differences for industries of fairly competitive market structure are not likely to be large, however.

---

onions, oilseeds, cotton, jute, sugar (raw), tobacco, milk, butter-oil, beef, mutton, wool, and hides and skins.

Unfortunately, it was not possible to include in this study all the industries that were covered by domestic price data. Several industries, such as cigarettes, have none of total supply imported, but none is exported, so there is no opportunity to observe prices either of imports or of exports. Quality differences make direct price comparisons very difficult, if not impossible, in both cigarettes and such industries as beverages or printing and publishing. These and similar industries are omitted from the averages.[1]

Indices of 'international prices' for manufactures are, for the most part, unit values of exports of major exporting countries. Some industries were covered by price information given by the United Nations, and some were taken from the trade statistics published by the OECD. Several indices used were averages of two or three leading countries' price or unit value indices. For some industries the unit value indices of imports of the commodity group into Pakistan have been used. The weights used for implicit exchange rates are the same as those used for domestic prices. Substantial variations in weighting for various estimates of sales and purchases by each sector did not result in very large differences in the behaviour of the weighted implicit exchange rates for each sector.

4. IMPORT LICENSING DATA

The data on import licensing composition from 1953 to 1964 were provided to the Pakistan Institute of Development Economics by the Chief Controller of Imports and Exports of the Government of Pakistan. These data were compiled and made available in mimeographed form by the Institute in its Research Report No. 35.[2] The data have been analysed and condensed into meaningful analytical categories in four studies. S. N. H. Naqvi has given a most useful compilation that was used in this monograph, in his Ph.D. Dissertation, *Commercial Policy and Resource Allocation* (Princeton, 1966).

[1] The manufacturing industries covered in the study were: ISIC Nos. 2092, 23, 24, 25, 27, 29, 30, 31, 32, 33, 34, 35, 36, 37, 38. Textiles (ISIC 23) were by far the most important industry, with cotton textiles first and jute textiles second in importance in terms of value added in manufacturing. The weighting system is discussed in detail in Lewis and Hussain, *op. cit.*

[2] S. N. H. Naqvi, A. M. N. Chowdhury, and P. S. Thomas, *Basic Statistical Tables, Import Licensing in Pakistan*, mimeographed, Karachi, 1965.

A short version of his major conclusions is given in 'The Allocative Biases of Pakistan's Commercial Policy'.[1] W. E. Hecox concentrated on the analysis of the commercial imports and the imports under

TABLE A-6. *Private Imports: CCIE Licensing and Actual Imports (Rs. million)*

Period (1)	*Commercial* (2)	*OCAC* (3)	*Industrial* (4)	*Bonus import* (5)	*Total CCIE licensing* (6)	*Actual private sector imports* (7)	*Col. (6) as percentage of Col. 7* (8)
Jan.–June 1953	—	—	—	—	74·6	—	—
July–Dec. 1953	—	—	—	—	309·8	—	—
Jan.–June 1954	—	—	—	—	311·9	—	—
July–Dec. 1954	153·9	—	94·9	—	248·8	506·6	49
Jan.–June 1955	213·6	—	90·6	—	304·3	415·6	73
July–Dec. 1955	221·7	—	163·0	—	384·7	522·2	74
Jan.–June 1956	227·9	—	178·7	—	406·6	467·6	87
July–Dec. 1956	312·6	—	106·3	—	418·9	515·7	81
Jan.–June 1957	104·3	106·9	133·1	—	344·3	503·7	68
July–Dec. 1957	128·5	100·0	171·1	—	399·6	463·3	86
Jan.–June 1958	134·8	81·1	186·2	—	402·1	476·3	85
July–Dec. 1958	117·7	106·7	159·1	—	383·5	465·4	82
Jan.–June 1959	125·1	105·1	161·2	16·1	407·5	374·3	109
July–Dec. 1959	152·5	108·7	221·7	60·2	543·1	692·5	78
Jan.–June 1960	156·9	107·3	215·3	70·7	550·2	989·4	56
July–Dec. 1960	231·8	107·4	269·6	72·6	681·4	1088·4	63
Jan.–June 1961	358·6	65·2	311·1	73·4	808·3	1032·4	78
July–Dec. 1961	280·5	102·3	363·8	81·8	828·3	1076·0	77
Jan.–June 1962	294·3	110·5	463·8	83·3	951·9	1182·9	80
July–Dec. 1962	326·8	107·1	411·3	109·3	954·5	1535·4	62
Jan.–June 1963	233·2	108·4	402·2	91·3	835·7	1264·4	66
July–Dec. 1963	288·7	108·4	382·7	110·9	890·7	1607·8	55
Jan.–June 1964	498·8	117·1	432·0	126·4	1174·3	1589·4	75

Source: Thomas, *op. cit.*

Bonus Vouchers in his Master's Thesis, *The Control and Composition of Commercial Imports in Pakistan* (Syracuse, 1967). Finally, the most thorough introduction to the subject of import licensing in Pakistan, which combines an analytical and historical review of

[1] *Pakistan Development Review*, Winter 1966.

policies with a quantitative analysis of licensing patterns by types of licences and by regions receiving licences is given by P. S. Thomas, 'Import Licensing and Import Liberalization in Pakistan'.[1] The principal trends in patterns of import licensing by type of licence (commercial, industrial, and Bonus Voucher imports, plus petroleum products issued to the Oil Companies Advisory Committee, or OCAC) are shown in Table A-6, which is taken directly from Thomas's article.

The principal limitations of the licensing data are that (i) they do not include the sanctions or licences for government or semi-government agencies, which are allocated through government ministries, and (ii) they do not include the allocation for private imports of machinery and equipment imported under sanctions from the investment licensing procedures of the government. Despite these drawbacks the licensing data provide a wealth of information for the analysis of government policy decisions. The data have not been tapped to the maximum extent as yet.

[1] *Ibid.*

Index

PROPER NAMES

SUBJECTS

For Product Safety Concerns and Information please contact our EU representative GPSR@taylorandfrancis.com
Taylor & Francis Verlag GmbH, Kaufingerstraße 24, 80331 München, Germany

www.ingramcontent.com/pod-product-compliance
Ingram Content Group UK Ltd.
Pitfield, Milton Keynes, MK11 3LW, UK
UKHW020203200926
475702UK00004B/587
* 9 7 8 1 0 4 1 2 4 9 8 3 2 *